# Best Practices in Reading

Improved Performance

LEVEL
**H**

*Options*
Publishing

A **Haights Cross Communications** Company

# TABLE OF CONTENTS

**Best Practices in Reading
Level H, Second Edition**

**Acknowledgments**

**Editor:** Paula Menta

**Senior Production Specialist:** Corrine Scanlon

**Senior Designer:** Deborah Diver

**Product Development:** The Quarasan Group, Inc.

**Cover Design:** The Quarasan Group, Inc.

pp 12–14 "Barnstorming Bessie Coleman" Adapted from ODYSSEY's February 1997 issue: Tuskegee Airmen, ©1997, Cobblestone Publishing Company, 30 Grove Street, Suite C, Peterborough, NH 03458. All Rights Reserved. Used by permission of Carus Publishing Company.

pp 124–126 "Human Code Machine" Adapted from ODYSSEY's January 1999 issue Codebreakers, ©1999, Cobblestone Publishing Company, 30 Grove Street, Suite C, Peterborough, NH 03458. All Rights Reserved. Used by permission of Carus Publishing Company.

ISBN-10: 1-60161-197-8
ISBN-13: 978-1-60161-197-0

Options Publishing
P.O. Box 1749
Merrimack, NH 03054-1749
TOLL FREE: 800-782-7300 • FAX: 866-424-4056

www.optionspublishing.com

# Bessie's Show

In the early 1900s, just seeing an airplane was a new and wondrous experience. Imagine the excitement of watching a pilot, nicknamed Brave Bessie, perform daring stunts with one of these marvelous new machines!

## Recognize Genre

Literature is classified by genre (ZHON-ruh), or type of writing. "Bessie's Show" is a story of **historical fiction**. Historical fiction stories are made up, but authors include facts about the time period. A character may be based on a real person, but many of the details are made up.

Think about another historical fiction story that you have read. Write the setting (when and where it takes place) and who the characters are.

Setting: _____

_____

_____

Characters: _____

_____

_____

## Connect to the Topic

Think about a time that you have seen stunt flying at an aerial show, on television, or in the movies. Describe what the airplanes can do.

_____

_____

_____

_____

_____

## Preview and Predict

Reread the introduction to "Bessie's Show." Look at the illustrations throughout the story. Predict why the pilot is nicknamed Brave Bessie.

_____

_____

_____

_____

_____

## STRATEGIES

**MAKE INFERENCES**
**MAKE CONNECTIONS**
**UNDERSTAND GENRE**
**VISUALIZE**

# Bessie's Show

**MAKE INFERENCES**

Authors don't always tell you everything. Use the details in a story and what you know to make an inference.

*I think people called her Brave Bessie because she performed daring stunts.*

Why would the people in the crowd show expressions of relief?

"Ah-choo!" a young boy sneezed as a strong gust of wind kicked up some dust. He stood in a cow pasture, **mesmerized** by the plane buzzing overhead. The small Curtiss Jenny plane, which people described as little more than a bunch of parts flying in formation, performed graceful figure eights over an amazed crowd. "Look at Brave Bessie go!" the boy exclaimed to no one in particular.

In the cockpit of the plane, the **aviator**, Bessie Coleman, laughed in delight as she straightened the plane. The young woman was doing exactly what she had always wanted to do. She was making her living as a **barnstormer**, which was quite unusual for an African-American woman in the 1920s.

Next, Bessie decided to attempt a stall. "Stalls always impress audiences," she thought. She positioned the plane directly over the crowd and turned off the engine. She imagined the collective gasp of the spectators as they heard the engine go silent, causing the plane to glide at only 45 miles per hour.

Bessie was low enough to detect expressions of relief as she restarted the engine. A blast of exhaust fumes hit her nostrils and a splat of oil sprayed out as she **coaxed** her Jenny to reach its top speed of 75 miles per hour.

**DID YOU KNOW?**

Many barnstormers were former military pilots. They bought old warplanes and used them to perform daring stunts.

**aviator** (AY-vee-ay-tuhr) a pilot
**barnstormer** (BARN-storm-uhr) in aviation's early days, a person who did stunt flying and gave short airplane rides
**coaxed** (KOHKST) gently increased the speed of
**mesmerized** (MEZ-muh-rized) in awe of; unable to look away

Brave Bessie entertained her admirers with more figure eights, barrel rolls, and dives. Then she prepared for the grand finale, which included a new feat. She had recently spiced up her show with parachute jumps to maintain the interest of her audiences.

Bessie examined the herd of cattle at the far end of the pasture. An advantage of flying over farmland was being able to use cows as weathervanes since the animals turn their tails to the wind. After checking the wind direction, she increased the altitude of the plane. "Ready?" she yelled over the engine's buzz to Eliza Dilworth, who was crammed into the miniature plane with her.

Eliza climbed out of the cockpit and cautiously crept to a large, canvas bag which was tied to the wing with a rope. The bag contained the parachute that would transport her to the ground. The woman **donned** the parachute, sat down on the wing, and jumped. "Snap!" went the rope that had secured the package to the wing. Eliza's parachute **billowed** open and floated her downward as the crowd stared in amazement.

The pilot watched with satisfaction and then circled back over the field, **scouting** for a suitable landing location. She decreased her speed, knowing the importance of coming in very slowly because the Jenny had no brakes.

**billowed** (BIL-ohd) swelled out
**donned** (DOND) put on
**scouting** (SKOWT-ing) observing carefully in order to obtain information

**VISUALIZE**

Use descriptions in a story to help you visualize expressions on a character's face.

Reread the first paragraph. Which details help you imagine the boy's expressions?

_____

_____

_____

_____

_____

What does this tell you about his feelings?

_____

_____

_____

_____

_____

_____

_____

The plane chugged safely to a stop. The boy who had been watching Bessie with **rapt** attention was the first to approach when she jumped out of the plane. His eyes sparkled upon seeing the woman in her aviator outfit. He could not contain his excitement as he blurted out, "I have to learn how to do that! It's the most exciting thing I have ever seen!"

Bessie smiled kindly and replied, "My dream is to start a flight school, but you are a bit too young to take lessons just yet. In the meantime, would you like to go for a ride?" Bessie expected the boy to agree eagerly, but instead he looked very disappointed.

"I don't have the five dollars," he said **dejectedly**, pointing to the poster advertising the fee for rides.

"What if I take you up for free and you pay me back when you become a famous aviator?" she offered with a twinkle in her eyes.

The boy's face broke into a huge grin as he said, "I'll be right back after I tell my dad where I'm going."

"Watch out," Bessie called after him, laughing. "Once flying is in your blood, it's almost impossible to get it out."

**THINK CRITICALLY**

Many people would envy Bessie Coleman's career as a barnstormer. Why do you think she thought it was important to start a flight school?

_____

_____

_____

_____

**dejectedly** (dee-JEK-tid-lee) in a depressed way

**rapt** (RAPT) completely absorbed

**Bessie's Show**

## Analyze Characters

A reader gets to know characters by what they say, do, or think. Think about how Bessie and the boy are alike and how they are different.

Use the Venn diagram below to compare the two characters. Write at least two details in each part of the diagram.

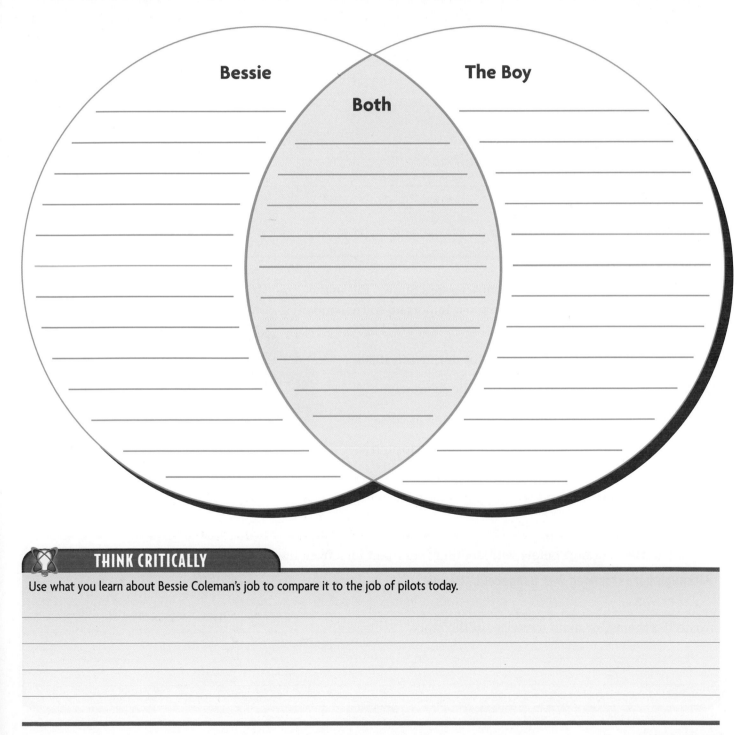

**Bessie**

**Both**

**The Boy**

---

**THINK CRITICALLY**

Use what you learn about Bessie Coleman's job to compare it to the job of pilots today.

## Summarize

Think about what it must have been like to be at the air show. Write a short summary of what happened in "Bessie's Show" from the boy's point of view.

_____

_____

_____

_____

_____

_____

_____

_____

_____

## Identify Details

Read the following list of details from "Bessie's Show." Fill in the bubbles for the three details that are most important to remember when retelling the story.

Ⓐ  Bessie Coleman was a talented pilot during the 1920s.

Ⓑ  One of Bessie's favorite tricks was the figure eight.

Ⓒ  Pilots could tell wind direction by looking at cows' tails.

Ⓓ  Crowds gathered to watch Brave Bessie perform tricks with her plane.

Ⓔ  Bessie Coleman inspired young people to want to fly.

Complete the sentence below with another important idea from the story.

**Although barnstorming was dangerous, Bessie** _____

_____ .

Write the theme, or main message, of the story.

_____

_____

_____

# Barnstorming Bessie Coleman

Bessie Coleman was born in 1892 in Texas, eleven years before the Wright brothers flew the first airplane. As a young woman, Bessie became fascinated with planes. She vowed that she would become a pilot even though no other African-American women had a license to fly.

## Recognize Genre

In a **biographical** sketch the author describes a person's accomplishments and certain events in his or her life. Identify a person you know and admire that you think would make an interesting subject for a biographical sketch. Tell one important event and one accomplishment of the person that could be included in the biography.

Person: _____

Important event: _____

_____

_____

Accomplishment: _____

_____

_____

_____

## Connect to the Topic

List three facts about Bessie Coleman that you learned from reading "Bessie's Show."

1. _____

2. _____

3. _____

## Preview and Predict

Reread the introduction. Look at the illustrations and captions throughout the selection. Predict which of the following is most likely to be the main idea of this biographical sketch.

(A) Many pilots in the 1920s became famous for their daring airplane stunts.

(B) Bessie Coleman became a talented aviator even though it was difficult for an African-American woman to do so in the early 1900s.

(C) Bessie Coleman never realized her dream of flying, but she is still respected for trying.

Which clues helped you choose your answer?

_____

_____

_____

Portrait of Bessie Coleman, the first African-American aviator in the world

**Barnstorming Bessie Coleman**

### STRATEGIES

**DRAW CONCLUSIONS**
**QUESTION**
**UNDERSTAND GENRE**
**MAKE CONNECTIONS**

### DRAW CONCLUSIONS

When authors don't state something directly, use details to draw a conclusion.

Why does the author say no one appreciated Bessie's accomplishments more than her mother?

_____

_____

_____

_____

_____

_____

_____

_____

_____

As Bessie Coleman's tiny plane swooped over Chicago in 1922, thousands of spectators oohed and aahed. Then they lined up for a ride. They had come to this air show because flying was still a **novelty**; the Wright brothers had made their first flight less than twenty years before. Many also wanted to meet Coleman, the first African-American woman to earn a pilot's license.

Probably no one that day appreciated Coleman's accomplishments more than her mother. An ex-slave, Susan Coleman had raised nine children alone in Texas after Bessie's father had left for Oklahoma. While most of the family picked cotton, Susan recognized Bessie's ability in math and assigned her the family's **bookkeeping** chores.

When Bessie wanted to go to college, her mother let her keep the money she earned from her job. Bessie could afford only one year's tuition. By 1917, she moved to Chicago and took a job as a manicurist in a barbershop. There she decided to become a pilot.

**DID YOU KNOW?**

In 1910, Blanche Stuart Scott was the first woman to fly solo. She never received a license.

**bookkeeping** (BOOK-keep-ing) making records of money received, owed, and paid
**novelty** (NAHV-uhl-tee) something new and unusual

Twenty-four-year-old Bessie receives a bouquet from a pleased Captain Edison McVey on Long Island.

Coleman could find no one in America to teach her to fly. She learned French, and with the help of Robert Abbott, editor of the *Chicago Defender* newspaper, sailed to France to study parachuting and stunt flying. After earning her international pilot's license in 1921, she returned to the United States determined to open a school for African-American aviators.

Like most pilots of the day, she was a "barnstormer" traveling around the country performing in air shows. (Organizers of these "flying circuses" often rented unused farmland for runways, and barns served as airplane **hangars**, thus the term "barnstormer.")

Coleman wore a leather helmet, goggles, long coat, and leather boots. Fans nicknamed her "Brave Bessie." After wowing mostly white crowds in the North, Coleman inspired African-American audiences in the South. On the side, she lectured at African-American churches and community centers. To raise money for her school, she also flew advertising by pulling advertising banners with her plane.

Despite the glamour, piloting **primitive** cloth-and-steel aircraft was a dangerous business. In 1923, Coleman finally bought her own plane, a World War I Curtiss JN-4 (Jenny). As she cruised to an exhibition in California, the motor stalled, and the plane plunged to the ground. "Brave Bessie" broke three ribs and a leg.

## QUESTION
Ask yourself questions about words or ideas you're not sure of.

*I wonder, why were air shows called "flying circuses"? The author says that people traveled around performing and entertaining an audience. I can see where it is very much like a circus.*

Write a question you have about the information in the biography.

_____
_____
_____
_____

Write the answer to your question.

_____
_____
_____
_____

## THINK CRITICALLY

How do you think African-American audiences felt when they heard Bessie Coleman lecture? What makes you think so?

_____
_____
_____
_____

**hangar** (HANG-ur) place to repair or house airplanes

**primitive** (PRIM-ih-tiv) simple or crude

## UNDERSTAND GENRE
(biographical sketch)
A biography tells about a person and his or her accomplishments.

What did you learn about the kind of person Bessie Coleman was?

_____

_____

_____

_____

Tell about one of her accomplishments.

_____

_____

_____

_____

_____

## MAKE CONNECTIONS
Bessie's courage and determination has motivated others to succeed. Write one thing that motivates you to succeed.

_____

_____

_____

_____

_____

_____

Young and determined, Bessie made her unique place in history and inspired many others.

From her hospital bed, Bessie sent a telegram to her fans: "Tell them all that as soon as I can walk I'm going to fly! And my faith in aviation and the [purpose]…it will serve in fulfilling the **destiny** of my people isn't shaken at all." Coleman knew that she was risking her life, but she said it was her "duty" to encourage African-American aviators. She refused to perform where African-American spectators were not welcomed.

In 1926, Coleman entered an air show in Jacksonville, Florida. Because no locals would lend or rent a plane to an African-American, Coleman asked her mechanic, William Wills, to bring her Jenny from Texas. On the morning of April 30, Wills piloted the Jenny over the field while Coleman sat in the back scouting sites for a parachute jump. She was not wearing a seat belt because she needed to lean over the edge of the open cockpit to see. All of a sudden, the plane flipped, hurling Coleman into a two-thousand-foot free fall that killed her. Wills died minutes later when the plane crashed.

Coleman never realized her dream of establishing an aviation school, but after her death Bessie Coleman Aero Clubs began to spring up. Bessie Coleman continues to motivate people because she proved that courage and determination can give wings to a dream.

### THINK CRITICALLY
How do photographs and captions help you understand this biographical sketch? What other kinds of graphic aids might help you understand even more?

_____

_____

_____

_____

**destiny** (DES-tuh-nee) the fortune or fate of someone or something

*Barnstorming Bessie Coleman*

## Identify Sequence

The biographer describes what and when things happened in Bessie Coleman's life. Putting these events on a time line can help you see how events are related.

Use the information in the introduction on page 11 and the biographical sketch on pages 12 through 14 to complete a time line of Bessie Coleman's life.

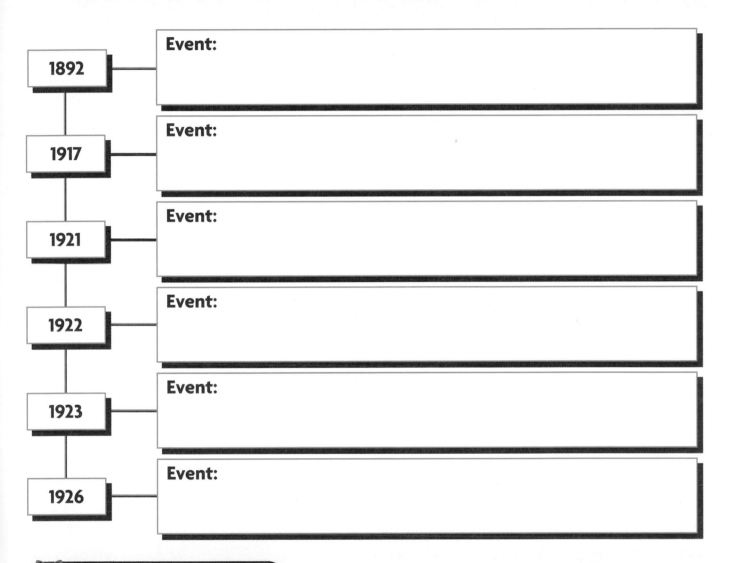

**1892** — Event:

**1917** — Event:

**1921** — Event:

**1922** — Event:

**1923** — Event:

**1926** — Event:

### THINK CRITICALLY

Biographical sketches cannot tell everything about a person's life. Tell what you think might have happened in her life between 1892 and 1917.

_____

_____

_____

*Barnstorming Bessie Coleman*

## Summarize

Some biographers have written entire books about the life of Bessie Coleman. Sometimes, however, writers of selections such as short encyclopedia entries or book descriptions must summarize the most important points about a subject in a paragraph.

Write a paragraph that summarizes the key points to remember about Bessie Coleman's life.

_____

_____

_____

_____

_____

_____

_____

_____

_____

## Identify the Main Idea and Supporting Details

Biographical sketches, such as this one about Bessie Coleman, provide interesting facts and details about a person. Real-life stories can also inspire readers with lessons about life. Complete the following sentences to tell what people can learn from reading "Barnstorming Bessie Coleman."

A lesson readers can learn from reading "Barnstorming Bessie Coleman" is

_____

_____

_____ .

Events from the biography that support this idea are

_____

_____

_____

and _____

_____ .

## Make Connections

Think about how "Bessie's Show" and "Barnstorming Bessie Coleman" connect to each other and to you. Answer the following questions.

1. After reading the biographical sketch about Bessie Coleman, why do you think she treated the boy the way she did at the end of "Bessie's Show"?

2. Which two facts about Bessie Coleman from the biographical sketch are also included in the story?

3. Bessie Coleman worked toward the goal of opening an aviation school. What is a long-term goal that you could work toward? Explain how you could achieve the goal.

4. Would you want to go an aviation school? Explain why or why not.

## Write an Interview

Imagine how exciting it would have been to talk with Bessie Coleman or someone else who flew in the early days of aviation. Write notes about questions you might ask about in a short interview with that person.

_____

_____

_____

_____

_____

_____

_____

_____

**BLACKLINE MASTER** Before you write, use the Blackline Master your teacher will give you to plan your interview.

## Plan Your Research

On the lines below, write some questions you would like to research about the history of aviation. Use print and online resources to find answers. Include what you find in your interview.

1. _____

_____

2. _____

_____

3. _____

_____

_____

**WEB CONNECTION**

http://www.OptionsPublishing.com/BestPracticesH

A man named Liu Xiang travels through Yellowstone with a geologist and a photographer. The tales that others tell about the natural wonders they've seen there seem unbelievable. Are the stories true, or just a fantasy?

## Recognize Genre

An author of **historical fiction** stories researches facts about a particular person or event in history. Then the author includes made-up details about what the characters might have felt, thought, and said during those events.

Think about an historical fiction story you have read. On the lines, write the name of the main character(s), the time period that the story took place, and an important historical event that happened.

Main characters:

_____

Time period:

_____

Historical event:

_____

_____

_____

_____

## Connect to the Topic

Reread the introduction to the story. Think about what you know about traveling to new places. Write two ideas about this below.

1. _____

_____

2. _____

_____

## Preview and Predict

Look through the story and think about what you know about the early days of photography. Why might a photographer travel to Yellowstone?

_____

_____

_____

## Land of Marvels

**QUESTION**

As you read, pause to ask yourself questions about what is happening in the story.

How will Jackson's photographs help Dr. Hayden?

Write another question.

---

When Liu Xiang reached the edge of the vast, beautiful canyon for the first time, he finally felt glad that he had joined the **expedition**. Traveling on a mule with a photographer and a **geologist** for three weeks had been exciting but difficult. The **terrain** was rugged. Each day they climbed steep rocks as they carried heavy equipment.

Originally, Liu had planned to head to California to work on the transcontinental railroad. But he also wanted to know if the rumors he'd heard about the Yellowstone area in the American West were true. Would they really see steam exploding from the earth or mud **seething** in boiling pools? Many stories were going around, but very few people had actually visited the area.

These natural wonders were exactly what the geologist, Dr. Hayden, hoped the photographer, a young man named William Henry Jackson, would capture for others to see. "I hope one day I'll persuade Congress to make Yellowstone a national park," Dr. Hayden had said to Jackson one evening. "Your photographs are my only real chance, Bill. The politicians back east just need to see this place to believe it."

"It's a great idea," said Jackson. The next day, Jackson walked up to Liu. "Liu, do you think you could help me and the other men carry my equipment? It's extremely heavy."

---

**expedition** (eks-pih-DIHS-uhn) trip made for a specific purpose

**geologist** (jee-AHL-uh-jihst) scientist who studies the rocks and soils of a place

**seething** (SEETH-ing) to move as if boiling

**terrain** (tuh-RAYN) the shape and arrangement of land; ground

Almost every morning from then on, Lui helped the other men carry the heavy equipment up the steep sides of the canyon. Jackson also gave Liu Xiang another job—to fire the flash powder that threw light into dark places so that Jackson could photograph them. When they entered dark, mysterious **caverns**, Liu would load the flash powder and set it off, creating a brief, blinding flare and a little smoke.

One hot morning in late July, Liu, Dr. Hayden, and Jackson loaded the photographic glass plates and chemicals into a boat. So far, Liu had seen many beautiful canyons and rock formations, but he wanted to see something truly **astonishing**.

Dr. Hayden, who had traveled in Yellowstone before, sensed this feeling in Liu. As he steered the boat with a wooden oar, Dr. Hayden murmured to his companions, "One of these days, gentlemen, we're going to see something that will leave you speechless."

The men floated past the towering rock walls and eventually reached a shallow area where trees lined the water. Liu was cleaning one of Jackson's plates in the warm water when he felt the bottom of the boat tremble. As the trembling grew more **insistent**, the boat shook.

Jackson firmly gripped the side of the boat. "What is that?" he said, looking around.

**DID YOU KNOW?**

Mineral deposits at Yellowstone's Mammoth Hot Springs create natural sculptures that resemble flowing water.

**MAKE CONNECTIONS**

To better understand historical fiction, it helps to compare details in the story to details in modern life.

What would you do today to use a flash on a camera?

_____

_____

_____

**DRAW CONCLUSIONS**

When an author doesn't tell you what a character thinks or feels, you can draw a conclusion from the way the character acts.

How did Jackson feel when he felt the boat tremble?

_____

_____

_____

**astonishing** (uh-STON-ish-ing) amazing; surprising

**caverns** (KAHV-urnz) large, underground caves

**insistent** (in-SIS-tunt) continuing to repeat; persistent

(historical fiction)
Authors of historical fiction make up characters' dialogue, thoughts, or feelings.

Although Jackson and Hayden were real people, some details are made up.

Write one detail about Jackson or Hayden that is most likely made up.

_____

_____

_____

_____

eerily (EER-ih-lee) strange and frightening

furrowed (FUR-ohd) wrinkled

geyser (GUY-zur) a spring that shoots hot water and steam

Dr. Hayden **furrowed** his brow, worried. He steadied the equipment with his hands. Liu sensed that something was about to happen.

Everything grew **eerily** silent, and the boat continued to shake. Once, back in China, Liu had lived through an earthquake, and it had begun with a similar trembling. Could there be an earthquake underwater?

Suddenly, about fifty feet away, hot water and steam shot up out of the water toward the sky. It was an incredible explosion of water and air.

"Wow!" said Liu. He could tell that water was boiling hot.

"Jackson," said Dr. Hayden, "get as many photos as you can!"

Jackson quickly coated his glass plate with chemicals. "I hope there's time!"

Luckily, the **geyser** continued shooting upward for about ten minutes. Incredibly, another geyser began just as the first one ended.

It was even more beautiful than Liu could have imagined!

Dr. Hayden named the first geyser "Grand Geyser," and the expedition—thanks to Jackson's photographs—was a success. The pictures proved that the tales of water shooting from the ground were true.

Hayden and Jackson returned to Washington, but Liu decided not to go with them. He chose instead to stay in the West, to see what other marvels there might be.

**THINK CRITICALLY**

Think about what the characters experienced at Yellowstone. Explain why Hayden wants to make Yellowstone a national park.

_____

_____

_____

## Identify Sequence

The sequence, or order, of events makes up the plot of a story.

Think about the events in "Land of Marvels." Use the flow chart below to write the sequence of events in the story. Two have been done for you.

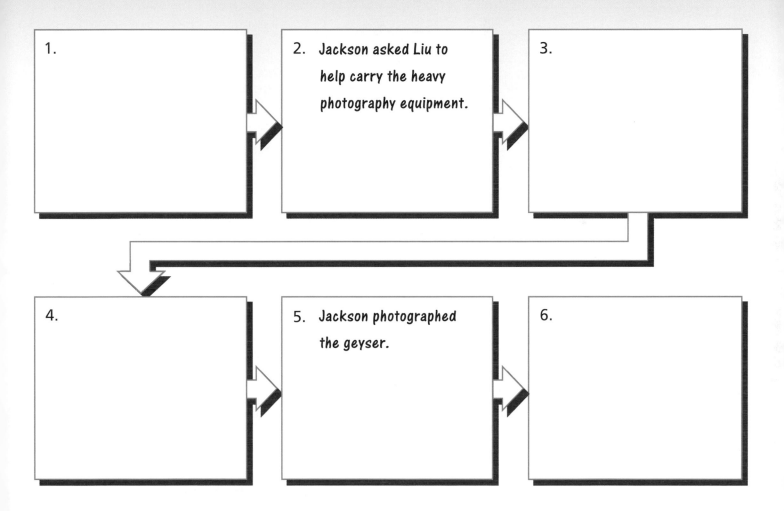

1.

2. Jackson asked Liu to help carry the heavy photography equipment.

3.

4.

5. Jackson photographed the geyser.

6.

### THINK CRITICALLY

What do you think might happen when Dr. Hayden and William Henry Jackson go to Washington to talk to Congress? Explain your answer with details from the story.

_____

_____

_____

## Summarize

Write a brief summary of "Land of Marvels." Organize the details by focusing on the goal of the expedition and how William Henry Jackson and Liu Xiang helped achieve that goal. Use the chart on page 23 to help you.

_____

_____

_____

_____

_____

_____

## Identify Theme

A theme is the main message, lesson, or idea about life that a story teaches. Which of the following best expresses the theme of "Land of Marvels"?

(A) "Practice makes perfect." If you do a job often enough, you will become good at it.

(B) "Don't cry over spilled milk." If something goes wrong, move on to the next thing.

(C) "Seeing is believing." People want proof before they will believe an incredible story.

(D) "Good work takes time." You shouldn't rush a job.

If you were to write a story about the Yellowstone area, what would your theme be? Explain your answer.

_____

_____

How did an isolated area, out West in the early days of this country, become America's first National Park? The old saying "seeing is believing" just may provide the answer.

## Recognize Genre

An **informational article** is nonfiction. Authors of informational articles often use headings to organize information. Turning a heading into a question can give clues about what is included in a section.

Look at the heading on page 26 of the article. On the lines below, write the heading and then create a question with it. Next, write what you think will be explained in that section.

Heading: _____

_____

Question: _____

_____

_____

Topic: _____

_____

## Connect to the Topic

Reread the introduction on this page. Think about what you learned about Yellowstone from reading "Land of Marvels." List two ideas below.

_____

_____

## Preview and Predict

Take a quick look at the title, photographs, and headings in the article. Fill in the bubble next to the best prediction about this selection.

(A) The article is about photography in 1871.

(B) The article is about how Congress turns a bill into a law.

(C) The article is about how Yellowstone became a national park.

(D) The article is about visiting a national park.

How and why did you choose your answer?

_____

_____

_____

Hayden Expedition camp on the edge of Lake Yellowstone in 1871

**STRATEGIES**

VISUALIZE
DRAW CONCLUSIONS
UNDERSTAND GENRE
QUESTION

A PLACE TO PROTECT

**VISUALIZE**

Authors include descriptions in an article to help readers imagine a place.

List the words and phrases that help you imagine the Yellowstone area.

_____

_____

_____

_____

_____

_____

_____

_____

_____

Native Americans called the place Yellow Rock River, probably because of the color of the sandstone **bluffs** that line a portion of the banks of the Yellowstone River. When explorers told stories about the area, many people refused to believe them. They said that it was a place where the earth rumbled and shook under their feet. Smoke **billowed** upward from cracks in the rocks, and enormous jets of hot water shot from the ground. Pools of boiling mud interrupted the landscape, and the river had cut a vast canyon with steep walls.

It all seemed too fantastic to be real.

## 1870: The Langford Expedition

To **scrutinize** the claims, Nathaniel Langford organized an expedition in 1870. When Langford returned from the Yellowstone area, he wrote a magazine article about what he had seen. The article was illustrated with drawings that were based on Langford's verbal descriptions to the artist.

Langford hoped that the United States Congress would vote to set the Yellowstone lands aside as a park for everyone to enjoy. But there was a problem. Many people were in doubt that the Yellowstone area was anything like Langford's description of it. Nonetheless, the idea of a national park that everyone could appreciate and enjoy was born.

The Yellow Rock River and the sandstone bluffs from which it gets its name

**billowed** (BIL-ohwd) rose in big waves
**bluffs** (BLUHFS) steep cliffs with straight walls
**scrutinize** (SKROOT-n-ize) to study closely; to inspect

Visitors can view Grand Prismatic Hot Springs in Yellowstone National Park from the nearby boardwalk.

**DRAW CONCLUSIONS**

Why was Jackson a good person to join the expedition that would convince Congress of the value of Yellowstone?

# 1871: The Hayden Expedition

Dr. F. V. Hayden decided to convince Congress to make Yellowstone a park by leading another expedition there to find and bring back **indisputable** evidence. Hayden was the head geographer and geologist of the United States. One of his jobs was to **survey** the territories that the United States had **annexed**. He had already seen Yellowstone, so he knew that its wonders were real. However, he needed evidence.

As William Henry Jackson wrote in his autobiography, *Time Exposure:*

That was where I came in. No photographs had as yet been published, and Dr. Hayden was determined that the first ones should be good. A series of fine pictures would not only supplement his final report but tell the story to thousands who might never read it.

**DID YOU KNOW?**

Jackson took over 400 shots of Yellowstone while on the 1871 expedition.

Hayden recruited Jackson for the expedition. Jackson had already made a name for himself with photographs of the American West, and this was not his first trip to Yellowstone. He knew what to look for, and he had a good idea of the kind of photographs that would prove the area was something special and should be preserved.

Hayden's expedition spent the summer of 1871 exploring the Yellowstone area. They returned with photographs that revealed a place even more amazing than the stories had made it seem.

**annexed** (UH-nexd) officially added new lands to an existing nation

**indisputable** (in-dih-SPYEW-tuh-buhl) cannot be denied; certain; unquestionable

**survey** (sur-VAY or SUR-vay) to examine closely and record the size, shape, and position of an area

Hayden and Jackson on the boat from which Jackson took some of his pictures

## UNDERSTAND GENRE
(informational article)
Informational articles have visual aids to help readers understand the text.

How do the photographs and captions support the article?

_____

_____

_____

## QUESTION
As you read, ask questions to make sure you understand facts and details of an article.

Why did some members of Congress think Yellowstone was worthless?

_____

_____

_____

# 1872: Success!

Meanwhile, back in Washington, Langford had run into some **aversion** to the idea of making Yellowstone a national park. Some people in Congress thought that Yellowstone seemed "worthless" because the area didn't have any **exploitable** resources. They didn't think Yellowstone was valuable.

When Langford explained the problem to him, the newly returned Dr. Hayden had an idea. Before the Yellowstone National Park bill came up for a vote, he placed a selection of Jackson's photographs on the desk of every member of the Senate and House of Representatives.

Jackson's photographs were persuasive. In 1871, people were not used to such images. A photograph was a remarkable thing, and the members of Congress had never seen photographs like these. Nor had they ever seen land like the place that the photographs showed.

Fortunately, Hayden's idea worked. After viewing Jackson's photographs, Congress voted in favor of making Yellowstone the first national park in the United States. Today, more than three million people visit the park every year. It seems that none of these people would consider the park's geysers, hot springs, waterfalls, and wildlife "invaluable."

Tower Falls in Yellowstone National Park

Jackson's photographs, such as this one of Giant Geyser, convinced Congress that Yellowstone's marvels were real.

**aversion** (uh-VUR-zhun) a feeling of strong dislike; opposition

**exploitable** (ek-SPLOYT-uh-buhl) useful in making a profit

## THINK CRITICALLY
Jackson's work had an important impact on our national park system. How might his work have affected the new field of photography?

_____

_____

_____

## Identify Cause and Effect

"A Place to Protect" explores how certain events led to the establishment of the Yellowstone area as a national park.

A cause is the reason why something happens. An effect is the result, or what happens. Read each cause in the chart below. Then reread the article and write the effect next to each cause.

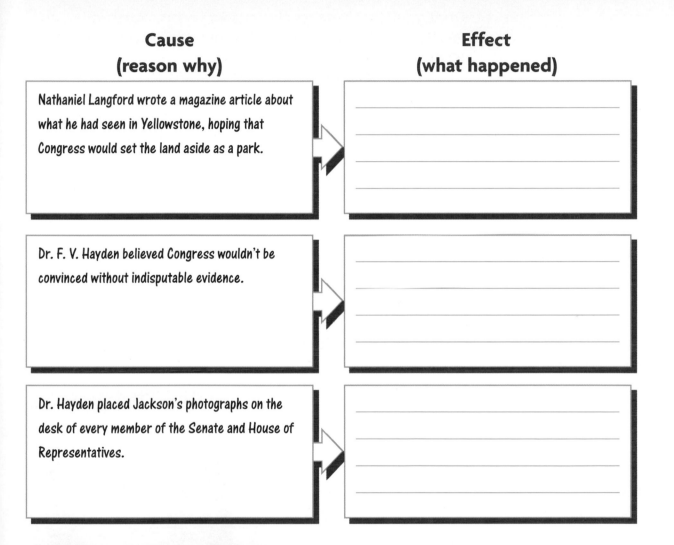

| Cause (reason why) | Effect (what happened) |
|---|---|
| Nathaniel Langford wrote a magazine article about what he had seen in Yellowstone, hoping that Congress would set the land aside as a park. | |
| Dr. F. V. Hayden believed Congress wouldn't be convinced without indisputable evidence. | |
| Dr. Hayden placed Jackson's photographs on the desk of every member of the Senate and House of Representatives. | |

### THINK CRITICALLY

The people who did not believe the drawings of Yellowstone did believe Jackson's photographs. Why were the photographs more persuasive?

_____

_____

_____

## Summarize

You learn new facts by reading an informational article. You can teach others what you learned by summarizing the most important facts and details in each section of the article.

Write a brief summary of "A Place to Protect." Use the information from the cause-and-effect chart on page 29 to help you.

_____

_____

_____

_____

_____

_____

_____

_____

## Identify Problems and Solutions

"A Place to Protect" tells how some individuals convinced people that Yellowstone should be made a national park. Read each problem below. Then write the solution to the problem.

**1.** How did Nathaniel Langford try to solve the problem of showing people what Yellowstone looked like?

_____

_____

What new problem did Langford's solution create?

_____

_____

**2.** How did Dr. Hayden try to solve the problem of showing people what Yellowstone looked like?

_____

_____

Why did that solution finally solve the problem?

_____

Old Faithful Geyser in winter

## Make Connections

Think about "Land of Marvels" and "A Place to Protect." Answer the following questions that connect the two selections to each other and to your experiences.

**1.** Which two facts from the article about Yellowstone were also included in the story?

_____

_____

_____

**2.** After reading both selections, why do you think W. H. Jackson agreed to go with Dr. Hayden on the expedition?

_____

_____

_____

**3.** After reading these two selections, what is your opinion about preserving land as a national park?

_____

_____

_____

**4.** What is one way Yellowstone National Park is similar to and one way it is different from a city or neighborhood park that you have visited?

**Similar:** _____

_____

**Different:** _____

_____

# Write a Newspaper Article

Imagine that you are a newspaper reporter in 1871. Write an article about the vote that created Yellowstone National Park. Use what you learned about the park from reading both selections. Answer the questions below to help you plan your article.

Who? _____

What? _____

Where? _____

When? _____

Why? _____

How? _____

**BLACKLINE MASTER** Before you write, use the Blackline Master your teacher will give you to plan your newspaper article.

# Plan Your Research

Research other national parks in your region of the country. Use print and online resources to find out why they were chosen to become national parks and what their unique features are. Take some notes below about what you learn.

The Mammoth Hot Springs are one of Yellowstone's main attractions.

_____

_____

_____

_____

_____

**WEB CONNECTION**

http://www.OptionsPublishing.com/BestPracticesH

## Dream Come True

Dori loves birds. She was disappointed when she was told that
only college students could participate in a program to help her feathered friends.
But Dori did not give up easily. She was determined to get involved.

## Recognize Genre

Details are important in **realistic fiction** stories.
Authors include details that are
true to life so their stories
seem real.

Read each pair of
sentences. Fill in the circle
next to the detail you might
find in realistic fiction.

1. Ⓐ A man travels back in time to prehistoric days.

   Ⓑ A man studies cave paintings to learn about
   prehistoric people.

2. Ⓐ A girl takes a wounded bird to the
   veterinarian.

   Ⓑ A sick animal tells the veterinarian what's
   wrong.

3. Ⓐ A family travels to the past to meet relatives.

   Ⓑ A family finds a large pumpkin in their garden.

Write another sentence that might be in a realistic
story.

_____

_____

_____

## Connect to the Topic

The introduction tells that a young teen wants
to get involved in a program to help birds. Ask
yourself, *"What are some tasks a person involved
in such a program might do?"* Write your ideas on
the word web.

count birds

tasks

## Preview and Predict

Reread the introduction and look at the illustrations
in the selection. Then fill in the bubble beside the
prediction that tells what will most likely happen in
"Dream Come True."

Ⓐ Dori will get involved in a program to help birds.

Ⓑ Dori will not get involved in a bird program.

Ⓒ Dori will start her own program.

Ⓓ Dori will help other animals because she is too
young for the bird program.

Why did you choose that answer?_____

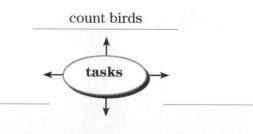

# Dream Come True

### STRATEGIES

**MAKE CONNECTIONS**
**VISUALIZE**
**UNDERSTAND GENRE**
**DRAW CONCLUSIONS**

---

**MAKE CONNECTIONS**

In order to understand what a character is feeling, think about your own experiences and how you would feel in the same situation.

> I felt just like Dori when I wanted to play on a softball team, but the coach said I was too young.

Tell about a time when you felt the way Dori probably feels.

_____

_____

_____

_____

_____

_____

---

The words gushed out as Alice described her work as a Project Puffin **intern** to her next-door neighbor, Dori. "The first day, Dr. Stephen Kress discussed how he established the program back in 1973 to help increase the puffin population. The small, black-and-white seabirds had been hunted for their feathers and meat until they were scarce. Dr. Kress brought puffin chicks to Hog Island. He also used **decoys** and recordings of bird sounds to trick puffins into believing that their kind already inhabited the island. Now there are over 80 pairs."

"I know. And now Dr. Kress' methods are being used to help other kinds of seabirds in Japan, Ireland, and other places," interrupted Dori.

Alice laughed, "*You* should be working at Project Puffin."

The girls' common love of birds, especially puffins, had sparked their friendship years ago. Since then, they had shared information and puffin **trinkets**. Dori was delighted that her friend was having this remarkable experience, but she also wished more than anything to be involved, too.

"Alice, you have *got* to get me into the program. Tell your supervisor that I'm a hard worker," begged Dori.

"You know that they only take college students as interns. You could go on a puffin sighting trip for younger kids," suggested Alice.

"No, I want to help puffins, not just look at them," Dori answered earnestly.

**DID YOU KNOW?**

In addition to decoys, Dr. Kress used mirrors in his work to make puffins think there were more birds present.

---

**decoys** (DEE-koys) artificial birds used to attract other birds

**intern** (IN-turn) a student undergoing practical training

**trinkets** (TRIN-kets) small, inexpensive jewelry

When she returned to work, Alice approached the project supervisor, Mr. Haskin, about Dori. He responded, "Sorry, the program is not open to middle-school students." Alice politely persisted, and eventually the supervisor offered, "Tell your friend that she can come and observe you tomorrow."

"Fantastic!" Alice answered.

"Tell her that it is very important that she not interfere with the workers, though," the supervisor added firmly.

When Dori arrived at the camp, Mr. Haskin greeted her and repeated his warning about not distracting the workers. Then he turned to Alice. "Please spend the morning in the bird **blind** working on counts and feeding habits. Dori, the work is **tiresome**, so you can watch Alice until you get bored, and then we will find something else for you to observe," he instructed.

Dori was thrilled to see puffins everywhere as she got settled in the blind. "How are you going to count them? There are so many, and they are in constant motion."

"I imagine a rectangle around part of the flock, count how many are in that group, then multiply that figure times the number of rectangles needed to cover the whole flock. It's called blocking," Alice explained and then got to work.

After a while, Alice turned her attention back to Dori, inquiring, "What are you doing?" Alice was surprised to see that Dori had been using blocking to count, and her numbers looked accurate. "Terrific job," Alice complimented her.

## THINK CRITICALLY

What does Dori do to show that she is truly interested in being in the program?

_____

_____

_____

## VISUALIZE

While you are reading, imagine what is happening. This helps you see characters more clearly.

What expression do you think Mr. Haskin has on his face as he talks to Dori? Why?

_____

_____

Authors often use dialogue to give the reader descriptive details. Use what characters say to help you visualize.

When Dori describes the birds as being in constant motion, I see them flying, walking on the sand, and fishing in the water.

If you were looking out from the blind with Dori and Alice, what would you see? Describe it.

_____

_____

_____

**blind** (BLIND) a shelter for hiding hunters, photographers, or observers of nature
**tiresome** (TIE-uhr-sum) tiring; boring

(realistic fiction)
In a realistic story, a character's thoughts, feelings, and actions should be like those of real people.

Why is it realistic that Alice offers to let Dori take some notes?

_____

_____

_____

_____

DRAW CONCLUSIONS

You can figure out a character's feelings based on what the character says and does.

> I can tell that Dori felt Mr. Haskin was angry with her because she stammered when he spoke to her.

What can you tell about Mr. Haskin's feelings from his words here?

_____

_____

_____

_____

banding (BAND-ing) putting strips of flexible material on the legs of birds for identification purposes

meticulous (mih-TIK-yuh-luhs) extremely careful

Next, Alice demonstrated how she recorded feeding habits. "Would you like to try it?" Alice asked. Dori eagerly agreed and spent the remainder of the morning taking **meticulous** notes.

After lunch, Alice was assigned to help with **banding**. Dori observed Alice and a volunteer, Jerry, set up a fine, black net to catch the birds.

"They get annoyed, but it doesn't injure them," Alice commented. Dori watched Jerry slip numbered aluminum bands onto the birds' legs and then release them.

"The bands help us track the activities of particular birds," Jerry explained. "Try it."

Dori couldn't believe that she was going to touch a puffin! She followed Jerry's directions exactly, slipping the band over the bird's leg.

"Great! Do some more," Jerry encouraged her.

Dori lost track of time as she banded birds all afternoon. As she released the last one, she heard someone approaching. Spinning around, she saw Mr. Haskin. "I hear that you have done a lot more than merely observe Alice's work," he said with a serious expression.

"Y-yes," Dori stammered, recalling how firmly he had cautioned her to stay in the background.

"We don't ordinarily include middle-school workers in our program, but you are an extraordinary worker. Please come back tomorrow," he invited with a smile.

"I'll be here!" Dori responded, beaming.

**THINK CRITICALLY**

If Mr. Haskin allows other middle-school students to join the project, how should he select them?

_____

_____

_____

*Dream Come True*

## Identify Story Elements

Realistic fiction, like all stories, includes the elements of character, setting, and plot. Many stories also have a theme, or message, that you can apply to your own life.

Review "Dream Come True" to help you complete the story map below.

**Characters:**

**Setting:**
Project Puffin on Hog Island

**Problem:**

**Main events:**

1. Alice tells Dori about her experiences as an intern, and Dori begs her to find a way she can get involved.

2.

3.

**Solution or outcome:**

### THINK CRITICALLY

Look over your story map. What is the theme, or message, of the story?

_____

_____

*Dream Come True*

## Summarize

Think about times when friends have told you about stories they have read. Sometimes, they leave out important information, and their summary is confusing. Other times, they tell too many details. To avoid these problems, you should base your summary on only the important points.

Use the story map on page 37 to write a short summary of "Dream Come True."

> I might need to include some background information about puffins because some readers of my summary may not know what they are.

_____
_____
_____
_____
_____
_____
_____
_____
_____
_____
_____
_____

## Analyze Characters

While reading a story, you learn about the traits of the main character. What were three important things about Dori that allowed her to make her dream of working with Project Puffin come true?

1. _____
_____
_____

2. _____
_____
_____

3. _____
_____
_____

# How to Make a Bird Life List

Have you ever thought about bird watching as a hobby? Birds come in a kaleidoscope of shapes, sizes, and colors. They have some interesting behaviors, too. Find out how to keep a "life list" of the fantastic flying creatures you observe.

## Recognize Genre

Most **how-to articles**, which explain how to do or make something, include both text and visuals. The visuals may include photographs, drawings, charts, or diagrams. They provide important information that shows what the words are telling the reader to do, or they provide additional information that is not included in the text.

Imagine you were writing a how-to article about something you know how to do. What would your topic be?

_____

List three visuals you might include in the article.

1. _____
2. _____
3. _____

## Connect to the Topic

Read the introduction to "How to Make a Bird Life List." Based on what you know about birds, what three important tips would you give for watching them?

**Tip 1:** _____

_____

**Tip 2:** _____

_____

**Tip 3:** _____

_____

## Preview and Predict

Reread the introduction and look at the visuals and headings in the article. Predict what you think a life list is and how it connects to bird watching.

_____

_____

_____

_____

_____

_____

_____

Bird watching can be an interesting activity for everyone in the family.

# How to Make a Bird Life List

## MAKE CONNECTIONS

As you read a how-to article, connect what the author says with your own experiences. This strategy will help you understand how to follow the directions.

*I have had lots of experiences with following directions. It's a bit like a recipe for cooking.*

How is this bird life list like a recipe?

_____

_____

_____

_____

_____

With very few materials and some simple tips about techniques, you can start a bird life list, a listing of all the birds you see in your lifetime.

**You will need:**
  small notebook for field notes
  pens or pencils
  colored pencils
  larger notebook for your life list
  **field guide**
  lightweight binoculars (optional)

## Preparation

**1.** Start a bird library. Collect field guides and other bird books, and visit birding sites on the Internet. Study these resources carefully to learn about the physical characteristics of various birds before you begin bird watching.

**2.** Consider collecting bird-song recordings to familiarize yourself with the sounds that different species make. This will also help you identify birds that you see.

**3.** Prepare life-sized outlines of birds to take into the field. These will give you a head start when you want to draw a bird you sight.

**DID YOU KNOW?**
The tiny bee hummingbird of Cuba weighs only about one-tenth of an ounce, while the ostrich found in Africa can weigh over three hundred pounds.

*A bird life list can include drawings of birds, as well as field notes.*

**field guide** (FEELD GIDE) a book that provides pictures and descriptions of animals or plants for the purposes of identification

# Setting Up a Life List

1. Set up a notebook for your life list. Start the first page with these column headings: *Species, Date Seen,* and *Location.*

2. Make a decision about the organization of your life list. Many people organize their lists by year so that they can compare how many and what types of birds they observe over time. As an alternative, you can set up your list geographically. That is, make a section for woods, seashore, city, and so on. Another option is to divide your list into sections for small, medium, and large birds. Of course, you should decide in advance how you will define each size before beginning your list.

Hummingbirds delicately sip nectar from flowers for food.

| Species | Date Seen | Location |
|---------|-----------|----------|
|         |           |          |
|         |           |          |
|         |           |          |
|         |           |          |

# Collecting Data for Your Life List

1. Determine where you will watch birds. Good **destinations** include farms, woods, beaches, marshes, areas around ponds and streams, quiet streets, windowsill birdfeeders, backyards, and city parks. The more variety you build into your bird watching locations, the more kinds of birds you are likely to see.

2. Once you are in your location, find an **unobtrusive** place from which to observe. For example, use hedges or trees as a natural blind.

3. To attract particular birds, you can use a recording of the sounds they make. Birds will be curious about these bird calls and come closer. But be careful! You want to avoid making noises that might startle the birds.

## QUESTION

Write questions you have as you read. Discuss them with others who have read the selection.

What question do you have about setting up a life list?

_____

_____

_____

Before you read a section of text, turn the heading into a question. This strategy will help you stay focused on the important information.

As I read "Setting Up a Life List," I'll look for the answer to this question: "How should I set up my life list?"

Write a question with this heading. Reread to find the answer.

_____

_____

_____

## THINK CRITICALLY

If you were going to set up a life list, how would you organize it? Why? You may wish to come up with your own way of organizing it.

_____

_____

**destinations** (des-tuh-NAY-shuhnz) places to which a person is going
**unobtrusive** (un-uhb-TROO-siv) not noticeable

A belted kingfisher with a fish it just caught

4. When you spy a bird that you want to record, look at it steadily for as long *as possible.* Memorize every detail of its size, shape, color, distinguishing marks, and actions. Don't look away until you are sure you have all the information you need.

5. When you are ready, use one of your bird outlines, along with your colored pencils, to draw the bird in as much detail as possible.

6. Finally, make meticulous notes in your field notebook. Write the species' name if you know it, location, date and time, weather, activities, and any other information you want to remember.

7. Continue using this process with each bird you wish to observe.

## Building Your Life List

1. When you return from a bird-watching expedition, review your notes and drawings as soon as possible.

2. Use field guides to research all the birds that are unfamiliar, to figure out their species. Some useful guides are *National Geographic Field Guide to the Birds of North America, All the Backyard Birds,* and *Stokes Beginner's Guide to Birds.*

3. Identify any subjects that are "life birds" for you—ones you have not observed before. Add these to your life list.

| Species | Date Seen | Location |
|---|---|---|
| mountain finch | 7/22 | Big Bear St.Park |
| common ground dove | 8/1 | Silver Lake |
| backyard puffin | 9/19 | Channel Islands |

## Learning More

Starting a bird life list can lead you in many interesting directions. Of course, you will want to continue building your birding library. You may also want to join a bird club or take birding expeditions with other **avid** bird watchers. An interest in birds could even lead you to a career in **ornithology**.

### MAKE INFERENCES
Authors of how-to articles do not explain the reason for every single step in their directions. Sometimes, you have to put together what the author says with what you already know to determine the reason.

Why do you think the author says not to look away from the bird?

_____

_____

_____

_____

### UNDERSTAND GENRE
(how-to article)
The purpose of a how-to article is to explain something.

Why does the author number the steps in each section?

_____

_____

_____

_____

**avid** (AH-vid) eager; very interested
**ornithology** (or-nuh-THOL-uh-jee) the scientific study of birds

*How to Make a Bird Life List*

## Identify the Main Ideas

The how-to article is divided into sections that explain different ideas about making a bird life list.

Write the main idea, or most important idea, of each section.

---

### Preparation

Main Idea:

⬇

### Setting Up a Life List

Main Idea:

⬇

### Collecting Data for Your Life List

Main Idea:

⬇

### Building Your Life List

Main Idea:

---

### THINK CRITICALLY

What patterns might you expect to find after a year of keeping a bird life list?

_____

_____

*How to Make a Bird Life List*

## Summarize

After you learn how to do something by reading a how-to article, you may enjoy teaching someone else what you have learned.

Write a brief summary that tells what you learned about making a bird life list. Use the chart on page 43 to help you.

> Because I'll be writing a summary instead of step-by-step directions, transitional words such as *first, next, then,* and *finally* will be important in making my writing clear.

## Identify Details

Read the following list of details from "How to Make a Bird Life List." Fill in the bubbles beside the three most important details to remember when retelling the how-to article.

(A) Bird watchers can use binoculars if they wish.

(B) Bird watchers use field guides to identify unfamiliar birds.

(C) Life lists help bird watchers keep track of all the birds they see.

(D) Some bird watchers organize their lists geographically.

(E) Taking specific notes is a key to being a successful bird watcher.

Yellow weaverbirds are named for their highly complex woven nests.

## Make Connections

Think about how "Dream Come True" and "How to Make a Bird Life List" are related to each other. Think about what you learned about birds and bird observations from reading these selections. Answer the following questions.

1. What bird-watching skills explained in "How to Make a Bird Life List" did Alice and Dori use in "Dream Come True"?

_____

_____

_____

_____

2. Do you think Dori would enjoy making a bird life list? Why?

_____

_____

_____

_____

3. How is making a bird life list similar to what the Project Puffin workers were doing? How is it different?

_____

_____

_____

_____

4. Write the names of two birds you have seen. How are they different? Write at least two examples.

_____

_____

_____

_____

## Write a How-to Explanation

Write a short how-to explanation about the process of blocking as Alice explained it in "Dream Come True." Use "How to Make a Bird Life List" as a model.

_____

_____

_____

_____

_____

_____

_____

_____

_____

_____

**BLACKLINE MASTER** Before you write, use the Blackline Master your teacher will give you to plan your explanation.

A cardinal in the wild will take on the vibrant color of the berries and pollen it eats.

## Plan Your Research

Build on what you learned about birds. List three questions you would like to research. Then use print and online resources to look up information about puffins or other birds.

1. _____

2. _____

3. _____

**WEB CONNECTION**

http://www.OptionsPublishing.com/BestPracticesH

Jamal has come to Africa to take photographs.
When he and his mother travel through Kenya, Jamal finds surprises at every
turn as he learns about the country and about himself!

## Recognize Genre

"Safari Journal" is an **adventure story** that is
told through the main character's journal entries.
In this type of **fiction**, the setting is real and the
events could happen, but the story is made up
by the author. In an adventure story, the main
character has an exciting or remarkable experience,
sometimes involving danger and risks.

Put a check on the line next to each feature you
might expect to find in an adventure story.

____ action                  ____ danger

____ mystery                 ____ close calls

____ historical events       ____ biographical details

Why is an adventure story believable?

_____

_____

_____

## Connect to the Topic

Reread the introduction to "Safari Journal." Ask
yourself: *What do I know about Africa? What
would people photograph in Africa?* List four
things you might expect a person to photograph.

1. _____

_____

2. _____

_____

3. _____

_____

4. _____

_____

## Preview and Predict

Look through the story. Think about the title and
the illustrations. Consider what you wrote about
the topic. Then make a prediction by completing
the sentence below.

In "Safari Journal," I think Jamal will

_____

_____

_____

_____

_____

**STRATEGIES**

**DRAW CONCLUSIONS**
**VISUALIZE**
**UNDERSTAND GENRE**
**QUESTION**

## DRAW CONCLUSIONS

Use clues in the story to help you figure things out.

Why was Jamal glued to the window?

_____
_____
_____
_____
_____

How do you think Jamal feels about Ansel Adams? What clues do you find?

_____
_____
_____
_____
_____
_____
_____
_____

**arid** (AIR-id) very dry

**Ansel Adams** (AN-sul A-dums) well-known American photographer who lived from 1902 to 1984

**safari** (suh-FAR-ee) journey over land, especially in Africa

Monday, July 10
Samburu National Reserve

I can't believe that I, Jamal Williams, am in Africa—Kenya to be exact. This has been my dream since I was three or four years old. Dad would tell me stories about our ancestors from Africa. The landscape is so different from California. And the wildlife is amazing! I was glued to the window as Mom and I were driven from the airport to the lodge. But I forgot to use my new digital camera. We saw several zebras. Our driver said they are Grevy's zebras. They're bigger than common zebras and have huge ears. Their bright stripes stood out sharply against the dusty, brown earth and pale-green bushes.

Tomorrow, we get up early for our first **safari** in the reserve. I can't wait to take pictures! Ever since I first saw **Ansel Adams'** photographs of Yosemite, I've wanted to capture Africa on film the way he captured the American West. Tomorrow, I will start!

Tuesday, July 11

Up at 5:45 A.M. for the first safari drive of the day. As we bumped along the reserve's dirt roads in the safari wagon, we saw gerenuk (GEHR-uh-nook), which are deer with long necks. They look like a cross between a deer and a giraffe. It's strange to see them feed. They stand on their hind legs and reach for leaves on the trees. We were close enough that I didn't even need to use the zoom feature on my camera.

**DID YOU KNOW?**
Located near the equator, Samburu National Reserve is hot and **arid**. Many kinds of animals live there, including cheetahs, giraffes, vervet monkeys, oryx, and crocodiles.

Over in a drying riverbed, a herd of buffalo with down-turned horns wandered along. They looked peaceful, though we were told they can be very dangerous. I said I'd like to see a group **charge**, and Mom gave me a look.

Just then we surprised a bull elephant from behind. Our driver **maneuvered** the wagon to its side and got past it, but another safari wagon almost ran into it. The guide said it's NOT a good idea to approach a bull elephant from behind. Mom covered her eyes while I took picture after picture.

We ended the drive with a sighting of a lioness and her two cubs. The mother looked very majestic laying in the brush with her two cubs around her. They didn't even look at us as we drove by.

It was great fun being out in the wagon, but I can't help feeling that the pictures I took are kind of ordinary. They don't really capture how exciting it is to actually be here! I want my pictures to be as effective as those of Ansel Adams.

### THINK CRITICALLY

When the guide warns Jamal and his mother about the animals they see, the two characters react differently. What does their behavior say about them?

**charge** (CHARJ) to attack
**maneuvered** (muh-NOO-vurd) guided skillfully

If you are not sure of something you read, ask a question about it. Then read ahead to see if you can learn the answer.

*I wonder, how do people get in and out of a village surrounded by thorny bushes? Maybe they leave a small opening during the day so people can come and go.*

What is a Samburu village like?

_____

_____

_____

_____

Why does Jamal mention Ansel Adams again?

_____

_____

_____

_____

_____

**predators** (PRED-uh-turz) animals that feed on other animals

**Wednesday, July 12**

This morning we visited a Samburu village. It was really incredible to see. The Samburu way of life hasn't changed in hundreds of years. The whole village is surrounded by thorny bushes piled five feet high to keep out leopards and other **predators**.

Inside were about 20 small huts. Our guide told us that about one hundred people live here. They will stay as long as there is good grazing for their animals. Then they will move to a new location.

On our tour of the village, we stopped where some young children were having school lessons. They were learning English and math as well as traditional Samburu ways.

Before I knew it, Mom was sitting on the ground surrounded by a group of five and six-year-olds, teaching them the ABC song. It was as if she were back in the U.S. with her kindergartners. The kids loved it, and I got some great pictures. I was grateful to spend some time with them. I learned about their way of life.

Suddenly, I realized that for me a place is not so much the land but the people. I love looking at Ansel Adams' photos of the landscapes of the American West, but my dream is also to focus on the people of Kenya.

## THINK CRITICALLY

Based on Jamal's journal, how is daily life in this part of Africa similar to and different from daily life where you live?

_____

_____

_____

## Analyze Characters

This story is told through the main character's journal entries, which describe his observations, thoughts, and feelings. Look back through "Safari Journal" to find the information you need to complete this character-study chart.

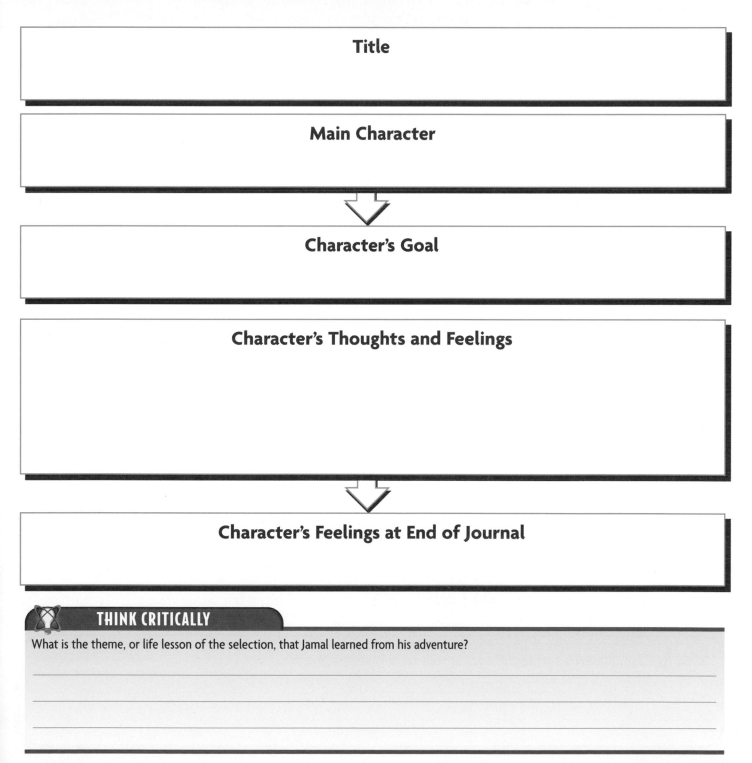

**Title**

**Main Character**

**Character's Goal**

**Character's Thoughts and Feelings**

**Character's Feelings at End of Journal**

**THINK CRITICALLY**

What is the theme, or life lesson of the selection, that Jamal learned from his adventure?

_____

_____

_____

_Safari Journal_

## Summarize

Suppose Jamal wanted to write a letter home to his best friend about what he was experiencing in Kenya. He would probably summarize the most important details from his journal entries. Write a brief summary of "Safari Journal." Use the chart on page 51 to help you.

_____

_____

_____

_____

_____

_____

_____

_____

_____

> I'll focus on how the safari affects Jamal. What does he want at the beginning? How do his feelings change? What changes them? I don't need to include all the descriptions of the things he sees. Those are details I can leave out.

## Identify Sequence

Think about the events that Jamal describes in his journal. Review "Safari Journal" and write the main events that took place in each entry.

Monday, July 10 _____

_____

Tuesday, July 11 _____

_____

Wednesday, July 12 _____

_____

What has Jamal learned from the events that took place?

_____

_____

# Man with a CAMERA

In "Safari Journal," Jamal Williams said he wanted to do for Africa what Ansel Adams did for the American West. What did Ansel Adams do? Read on to find out.

## Recognize Genre

**Nonfiction** is writing that gives facts about real people, places, and things. It is the opposite of fiction, in which characters and events can be made up by the author. The nonfiction you are about to read is a **biographical sketch**. A biography is a person's life story written by someone else. A biographical sketch is shorter than a full-length biography.

Nonfiction pieces have features that are not usually included in works of fiction. Nonfiction may be divided into sections with headings. It may be illustrated with photographs, charts, or graphs.

Look through "Man with a Camera." Then circle each feature that the biographical sketch contains.

| | | |
|---|---|---|
| drawings | headings | chart |
| captions | time line | photographs |

What other features do you often find in nonfiction pieces?

_____

_____

_____

## Connect to the Topic

Reread the introduction to "Man with a Camera." Recall what Jamal said about Ansel Adams in "Safari Journal." Ask yourself: *What do I already know about Ansel Adams?* Fill in the bubble next to each fact that you have already learned about Ansel Adams.

(A) Ansel Adams took photographs of landscapes.

(B) Ansel Adams used a digital camera.

(C) Ansel Adams took a lot of photos of the American West.

(D) Ansel Adams became a photographer late in life.

Write one idea you know about photography.

_____

_____

_____

## Preview and Predict

Think about the title, the introduction, and the features of this biographical sketch. Predict one thing you think you will learn about Ansel Adams as you read "Man with a Camera."

_____

_____

_____

Sierra Club lodge, photographed by Ansel Adams in Yosemite National Park, California

**UNDERSTAND GENRE**
(biographical sketch)
In a biographical sketch, there aren't enough pages to tell every detail about a person's life. The author must select facts that support the main idea.

Since the title is "Man with a Camera," the sketch must have something to do with Ansel Adams' decision to become a photographer.

What is another feature of a biographical sketch on this page?

_____

Why did the author include it?

_____
_____
_____

# Man with a CAMERA

## A Visit to Yosemite

Sick in bed at the age of 14, Ansel Adams looked through a book about Yosemite Valley, located about 150 miles east of his San Francisco home. "That's where I want to go on vacation this year," he told his parents. So on June 1, 1916, the three of them set off for a month of exploring the majestic scenery of Yosemite. Soon after they arrived, Ansel's parents gave him a **box camera.** Hiking and photographing in the Sierra Mountains was the perfect outlet for this **inquisitive** teenager's high energy.

Ansel was a bright child, but school was not easy for him. He was more interested in doing his own exploring, rather than following a set way of doing something. When he was 12, his parents decided to school him at home. His special love was music, and he **diligently** studied the piano.

The vacation in Yosemite awakened Ansel's interest in photography and began a lifelong appreciation for the area. When he returned to San Francisco, he got a job as a "darkroom monkey," doing odd jobs at a photo lab and also learning to develop and print photos. Summer after summer he returned to Yosemite to hike and take photographs. For several summers, he had a job as caretaker of the Sierra Club's lodge in the park.

**box camera** (BOX CAM-ruh) an old-fashioned camera shaped like a box

**diligently** (DIL-uh-juhnt-lee) with careful, steady effort

**inquisitive** (in-KWIZ-uh-tihv) curious; full of questions

# Ansel Adams

| 1902 | 1914 | 1916 | 1927 | 1928 |
|------|------|------|------|------|
| Born in San Francisco | Teaches himself to play the piano | Takes pictures with his first camera on family trip to Yosemite National Park | Takes the photo "Monolith," The Face of Half Dome; publishes his first portfolio, *Parmelian Prints of the High Sierras* | Marries Virginia Best in Yosemite |

Ansel Adams captures the stunning beauty of Half Dome, a mountain in Yosemite National Park.

**DID YOU KNOW?**

Photography had already come a long way by 1927. When the first photograph was taken in 1826, the photographer exposed the plate for eight hours to capture an image.

## A Moment of Truth

Ansel became more and more absorbed in his photography, but he still planned on a career as a concert pianist. This was mostly because he was not convinced that he could express emotions through photography as well as he could through music.

That all changed one spring day in 1927. Hiking in Yosemite with his **cumbersome** photographic equipment, Ansel found himself high on a cliff with a view of Half Dome, a famous mountain in the park. In those days, serious photographers used large, coated-glass plates instead of film to capture images. Ansel had just two unexposed plates remaining. With one of them, he took a typical shot of the mountain. Then he was inspired to do something different. In his own words: " . . . that was the first time I realized how the print was going to look—what I now call visualization—and was actually thinking about the emotional effect of the image . . . I began to visualize the black rock and deep sky. I really wanted to give it a monumental, dark quality. So I used the last plate I had with a No. 29-F red filter . . . and got this exciting picture."

Within a few years of this **epiphany**, Adams gave up the idea of becoming a concert pianist and devoted himself wholeheartedly to photography. He became one of the most well-known and respected photographers of his time.

**MAKE CONNECTIONS**

When reading nonfiction, relating to events in the text can help you understand it better.

Adams knew what he wanted his picture of Half Dome to look like before he took the picture. He "saw" it in his mind. Write an example of how visualizing can help you with a school project.

_____

_____

_____

When you read about people, think about what you have in common with them.

Adams was pleased when the photo he "saw" in his mind came out on film the way he had imagined it. Write about a time you were surprised by something turning out better than you expected.

_____

_____

_____

| 1934-1971 | 1940 | 1946 | 1965 | 1980 | 1984 |
|---|---|---|---|---|---|
| Serves on Sierra Club Board | Helps found Department of Photography at Museum of Modern Art, New York City | Receives Guggenheim Fellowship to photograph national parks | Named to President Johnson's environmental task force | Awarded Presidential Medal of Freedom by President Carter | Dies on April 22 |

**cumbersome** (KUM-bur-sum) hard to handle

**epiphany** (ih-PIF-uh-nee) moment of sudden understanding

QUESTION

Ask yourself questions when you are not sure of something. Reread or read ahead to find an answer.

I'm not sure why Ansel Adams worked with black-and-white images instead of color.

Write a question you have about Adams' approach to photography. Reread to find the answer.

_____

_____

_____

_____

_____

In the first paragraph, what does it mean to say that photography is "too realistic to be an art form?"

_____

_____

_____

_____

**convey** (kuhn-VAY)
to get the idea across; to tell

**external** (eks-TUR-nuhl) having to do with the outside

# A New Approach

In the early years of the twentieth century, photography was considered too realistic to be an art form. Photographers tried to make their photographs look like paintings by using soft-focus lenses, applying brush strokes to negatives, and printing their images on soft-textured paper.

Ansel Adams and others came to disagree with this kind of photography. They developed a style, known as "straight photography," which used sharp focuses and images printed on glossy paper. Adams used this style to capture the emotional reality behind the **external** scene. He also worked with black-and-white images, rather than color. He felt this focused the viewer on the emotional content of the scene, instead of on the external reality of what was being shown.

# Champion of the Environment

Throughout his life (1902-1984), Ansel Adams continued to take photographs of the American West. He became closely involved with the Sierra Club, an organization devoted to the protection of wilderness areas, and he frequently used his photographs to **convey** the message that the wilderness must be preserved.

Ansel Adams stands on a bluff above the Pacific Ocean.

After his death, in 1984, the United States Congress established the Ansel Adams Wilderness Area, southeast of Yosemite National Park. In 1985, a mountain on the southeast border of Yosemite was named Mount Ansel Adams in his honor.

## THINK CRITICALLY

What kinds of emotions might be conveyed through nature photography?

_____

_____

Why might a conservation group want viewers to feel certain emotions when they look at nature photos?

_____

_____

## Identify the Main Ideas and Supporting Details

The biographical sketch of Ansel Adams contains four sections. Each section develops one main idea with supporting details. Complete the chart below by writing the main idea and one supporting detail for the sections noted.

### A Visit to Yosemite

Main Idea:

Supporting Detail:

### A Moment of Truth

Main Idea:

Supporting Detail:

### A New Approach

Main Idea:

Supporting Detail:

### Champion of the Environment

Main Idea:

Supporting Detail:

### THINK CRITICALLY

Think about what you learned in "Man with a Camera." Write the main idea, or most important idea, of the biographical sketch.

## Summarize

If someone asked, "Do you know anything about Ansel Adams?" you might answer by giving a summary of "Man with a Camera." A summary contains the most important ideas from a piece of writing.

Summarize "Man with a Camera." Use the chart on page 57 to help you identify some important ideas.

_____

_____

> To summarize this biographical sketch, I should write the most important events in Ansel Adams' life in my own words.

_____

_____

_____

_____

_____

_____

## Identify the Main Idea and Supporting Details

If you wanted to share with someone the most important information you know about Ansel Adams, you would focus on main ideas. Sometimes, however, people are also interested in details. Details give a fuller picture of the main idea. It's important to be able to distinguish between the main ideas and the details.

Read each sentence below. Write **M** next to the main ideas of a section and **D** next to the details that tell more about a main idea.

_____ Ansel Adams was sick in bed when he got the idea for his family to visit Yosemite.

_____ Ansel Adams used photography to express emotion.

_____ Ansel Adams took care of the Sierra Club lodge in Yosemite during the summer.

_____ A mountain is named in honor of Ansel Adams.

_____ Ansel Adams used his photos to promote the protection of the environment.

A replica of the first camera given to Ansel Adams by his parents

## Make Connections

Think about how "Safari Journal" and "Man with a Camera" connect to each other and to you. Answer the following questions.

1. Jamal Williams was inspired by the work of Ansel Adams. In what ways were his ideas similar to Adams'? In what ways were they different?

_____

_____

_____

_____

2. If you were going to document one special part of your world, as Ansel Adams did the American West and Jamal Williams did Africa, what part would you choose? Explain why.

_____

_____

_____

_____

3. What might Jamal ask Ansel Adams if he had the opportunity to speak with him? Why would he ask these questions?

_____

_____

_____

_____

4. Ansel Adams wanted to preserve the wilderness areas in the American West. What part(s) of the world do you feel should be preserved for all people to enjoy? Explain why.

_____

_____

_____

_____

# Write a Journal Entry

In "Safari Journal," the character Jamal Williams describes his experiences—what he sees, does, and feels—in journal entries. Write a journal entry that describes an experience you have had. Describe events and images as well as your feelings about them.

Journal Entry Date: _____

_____

_____

_____

_____

_____

_____

**BLACKLINE MASTER** Before you write, use the Blackline Master your teacher will give you to plan your journal entry.

# Plan Your Research

Write three questions you have about Kenya, the Samburu, photo safaris, Ansel Adams, or Yosemite. Use resources in the library or online to help you research the answers.

*Adams inspired photographers to convey emotion through black-and-white photography.*

1. _____

_____

2. _____

_____

3. _____

_____

**WEB CONNECTION**

http://www.OptionsPublishing.com/BestPracticesH

# It's Just My Job

Some people see Marisa Montero as a hero because of her profession.
Marisa simply sees herself as a person doing her job.

## Recognize Genre

In every **adventure story** is an element of danger. Characters must deal with risky and unexpected events as the story unfolds. They can find adventure in their travels or in their jobs.

List two jobs that you consider adventurous. Then tell why you consider them to be risky.

| Adventurous Job | Why It's Risky |
|---|---|
|  |  |
|  |  |

## Connect to the Topic

Reread the introduction on this page. The main character of the story is a special kind of firefighter. Think of what you know about fighting fires. Circle **T** for true or **F** for false for the statements below.

T   F   Firefighting can be a dangerous job.

T   F   It is more important to be an independent worker than a team player as a firefighter.

T   F   People who enjoy fighting fires probably would not be happy working at desk jobs.

T   F   Firefighters are usually appreciated for their work.

## Preview and Predict

Look at the illustrations in "It's Just My Job." What kind of firefighter do you predict is the main character? Which clues helped you make your prediction?

**Prediction:** _____

_____

_____

_____

**Clues:** _____

_____

_____

_____

**It's Just My Job**

## STRATEGIES

**QUESTION
UNDERSTAND GENRE
VISUALIZE
MAKE INFERENCES**

### QUESTION

To learn more about characters, ask yourself questions about how they behave.

Why is Marisa surprised by the reporter's question?

_____

_____

_____

Ask yourself questions when you're not sure of something. Reread or read ahead to find answers.

Write a question about the events on this page.

_____

_____

_____

"I have one more question," the television news reporter said to Marisa Montero as she stood outside the ranger station. "Being a **smokejumper** is risky. Why do you do it?"

Marisa had answered all the interviewer's questions about the fire at Lake Arrowhead with ease, but this query caught her by surprise. She hesitated a moment and then said, simply, "It's just my job."

The camera shifted to the reporter, who ended the interview with, "This is John Maxwell for San Bernardino's KVCR, wishing you a good day."

The reporter shook hands with Marisa and the other firefighters who had participated in the interview. Marisa realized that she was exhausted. Almost a week ago, she had been eating lunch with a friend, who was also a smokejumper, when a siren blast called them to report for duty.

For several days, a ground crew had been fighting the slow-burning fire at Lake Arrowhead that a careless camper had started. Fortunately, a steady wind was pushing the blaze south toward the lake. When it reached the water, it would naturally burn out. Marisa was surprised that smokejumpers were being called in for such a routine fire.

### DID YOU KNOW?

In 1919, fire patrols began flying over national forests to locate forest fires, but the first smokejumpers didn't start battling blazes until 1940.

**smokejumper** (SMOHK-juhmp-uhr) a firefighter who jumps from an airplane into remote wilderness areas to control forest fires

When the call came in the lunchroom, Marisa and the other jumpers sprinted to the nearby locker room, where they put on jumpsuits and heavy boots. Their tools and parachutes had already been loaded onto the plane. Within fifteen minutes, the plane was taking off. Marisa's supervisor explained that the winds were **accelerating**. As the fire became stronger, burning **embers** were shooting off and starting new fires in areas that the ground crews could not reach. With a more intense fire came the danger of **crown fires**. Now Marisa understood why jumpers had been called in.

The plane soon arrived above the scene of the fire. To determine air direction and speed, the supervisor tossed a weighted crepe-paper streamer out of the plane. This data helped the smokejumpers parachute accurately to a location near, but not in, the fire. At her supervisor's direction, Marisa tucked in her chin, pushed out of the plane, and floated toward the forest with the other firefighters. Parachutes with packs of tools attached also descended into the forest. Upon landing, Marisa immediately smelled the choking smoke and heard the train-like roar of the fire.

Marisa quickly removed her jumpsuit and parachute and got to work. After a few hours of attempting to tame the smaller wildfires in the area, Marisa made a frightening discovery. "The wind has changed! It's blowing toward the east!" she yelled to the leader.

## UNDERSTAND GENRE

(adventure)

List three risky situations that the author has included so far.

1. _____

_____

2. _____

3. _____

## VISUALIZE

As you read, imagine what is happening. This helps you get a better understanding of the story.

I can picture Marisa racing out of the lunchroom to get herself ready for the flight to the fire. She is moving fast and looks very serious.

What do you visualize happening on this page?

_____

_____

_____

## THINK CRITICALLY

Write a fact Marisa might tell about her job.

_____

_____

Write an opinion she might give about her job.

_____

_____

**accelerating** (ak-SEL-uh-rayt-ing) picking up speed

**crown fire** (KROUN FYE-er) a fire burning hot enough to continuously spread through the tops of trees

**ember** (EM-ber) a glowing coal from a fire

This was a serious turn of events, because it meant that the fire was now heading toward cabins, lodges, and recreational areas. Now, the blaze would not burn its way to the lake. It had to be stopped before it reached the resort area!

The firefighters began the backbreaking task of establishing a **fireline**. They worked non-stop for two days, clearing a path that they hoped would stop the ferocious wall of flame. Their hard work paid off. The fire roared up to the fireline. With relief, the jumpers saw that the fire was not going to cross the line. As the firefighters watched from across the fireline, it began to rain. At first, it was just a slow drizzle, but within a couple of hours it turned into a steady, soaking downpour.

Once the rain stopped and they could see that the flames were extinguished, the jumpers unrolled their sleeping bags and got a few hours of rest. When they awakened, the leader announced, "It's time to check for hotspots." The smokejumpers got down on their hands and knees and felt every inch of ground to make sure it was cool.

After two days of **mop-up** operations, the firefighters were confident that the fire was out. The leader radioed for a helicopter to pick them up. They had been in the woods fighting the fire for five days with very little rest. As they waited for the helicopter to land, Marisa thought how good it was going to feel to shower and fall into her bed.

## MAKE INFERENCES

Use what you already know to figure out what the author doesn't explain.

*I can infer that people live nearby because I read about cabins and lodges.*

How might the firefighters feel when it starts to rain? Why do you think so?

What does feeling the ground tell about fire?

## THINK CRITICALLY

Suppose this story was told from the point of view of someone who lived in one of the nearby cabins. How would the details be the same? How would they be different?

**fireline** (FYE-er-line) a path along which all burnable materials are removed to stop a fire

**mop-up** (MOP-UHP) a putting out of the last embers and coals of a fire

*It's Just My Job*

## Identify Plot

Adventure stories usually have turning points. Just when the reader is wondering how the characters will ever be able to solve their problem, something happens to change the situation.

Review "It's Just My Job." Then complete the chart below by writing the most important events that make up each part of the story.

I have to think about where the adventure began. In this story, it did not begin right away.

### "It's Just My Job"

**1. Events at the beginning of the story:**

_____

_____

_____

_____

**2. Turning point:**

_____

_____

_____

_____

**3. Events at the end of the story:**

_____

_____

_____

_____

### THINK CRITICALLY

What is the theme, or main message, of "It's Just My Job"?

_____

_____

_____

_____

## Summarize

A story summary includes the important events of a story. It tells what happened, why, when, and where it happened, and who was involved.

Summarize "It's Just My Job" by answering the questions below.

What happened? _____

_____

Why? _____

_____

When? _____

Where? _____

Who was involved? _____

## Identify Plot

Many details that adventure story authors include are used to develop the action of a story. Other details make the story colorful and interesting, but are not important parts of the action. Fill in the bubbles beside the four details that are important to the action of the story.

(A) Marisa was having lunch with a friend.

(B) Smokejumpers can get to fires that ground crews cannot.

(C) The steady wind became stronger.

(D) The paper that the supervisor threw out of the window was crepe paper.

(E) The wind started to move the fire toward the resort.

(F) Rain helped put out the fire.

(G) The reporter who interviewed Marisa was from San Bernardino.

Write two more details that are important for retelling the story.

_____

_____

_____

# Let It Burn?

In recent years, there have been about 59,000 to 91,000 annual wildfires in the United States. Debates rage among people over whether wilderness fires are a tragic loss or a benefit to nature.

## Recognize Genre

Some **informational articles** contain both facts and opinions. A fact is a statement that can be proven. An opinion is someone's idea or belief about those facts, which is not necessarily true and cannot be proven. This article presents arguments for and against wilderness fires. The opinions and facts support the arguments.

Decide which statements below are facts and which are opinions. Write **F** or **O**.

_____ Forest fires are scary.

_____ A firefighter goes through training.

_____ Fires spread in a forest.

_____ Everybody loves Smokey Bear.

A serious wildfire damaged Yellowstone National Park in 1988.

## Connect to the Topic

Read the introduction on this page. Think of what you know about forest fires. Fill in two causes and two effects on the chart.

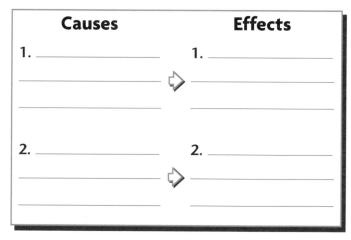

| Causes | Effects |
|--------|---------|
| 1. _____ | 1. _____ |
| 2. _____ | 2. _____ |

## Preview and Predict

Reread the introduction and look through the article. Make a prediction. What do you think you will learn about the debate over whether wildnerness fires are tragic or beneficial?

_____

_____

_____

_____

_____

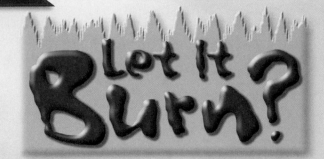

### STRATEGIES

**VISUALIZE**
**UNDERSTAND GENRE**
**MAKE CONNECTIONS**
**MAKE INFERENCES**

---

**VISUALIZE**

As you read, try to imagine what is being described to better understand the text.

How might a section of forest look after this kind of fire?

_____

_____

_____

_____

Which words help you visualize the fire in Los Alamos, New Mexico?

_____

_____

---

**debris** (duh-BREE) broken remains; litter

**prescribed burns** (prih-SKRIBED BURNZ) intentionally set fires to eliminate burnable debris

**rejuvenate** (rih-JOO-vuh-nayt) to make young again

**run amuck** (RUN uh-MUHK) to get out of control

**underbrush** (UN-dur-brush) small trees or bushes

---

"Only you can prevent wildfires," is Smokey Bear's message. This highly recognizable character has been campaigning against forest fires since 1944. Preventing these fires is important to preserving the wilderness and to saving lives. Why, then, do a growing number of scientists actually want to let some wildfires burn?

Odd as it may seem, forest fires can actually be beneficial. They act like forest vacuum cleaners and rid areas of flammable **debris**, such as dead limbs and **underbrush**. They temporarily reduce disease, weeds, and insects. Forest fires also recycle nutrients into the soil to **rejuvenate** forests and encourage growth of new vegetation. For these reasons, some people argue that forest fires should be allowed to burn. Sometimes they even start fires, called **prescribed burns**.

In 2004, a prescribed burn in the Loxahatchee National Wildlife Refuge in Florida helped stop the spread of a wildfire that was started by lightning. The wildfire fizzled out when it reached the area where the prescribed burn had been done. The home of hundreds of bird species was saved.

Not everyone agrees that forest fires are good. Opponents of natural fires and prescribed burns are quick to point out that when forest fires **run amuck**, the results are tragic. They point out a parkland fire that ran wild after it started as a prescribed burn a few years ago in Los Alamos, New Mexico. That fire caused one billion dollars of damage, including the loss or damage of 44,000 acres of land, 260 homes, and 1,500 archeological sites.

There is also the threat of danger not only to land and homes, but to the people who live near the fires and the firefighters who risk their lives putting them out. The danger does not end when the fire goes out and the mop-up operations are completed. Air pollution, landslides, floods, erosion and possible damage to the ozone layer can all result from fires left to burn.

Some experts claim that no matter how much care and preparation is involved, there is always an element of risk with prescribed burns. Not only is there the chance that a fire can get out of control, but plant and animal populations can be negatively affected. Experts also point to studies that show decreased numbers of herb plants and animals, such as millipedes and certain ant and beetle species.

People in favor of the idea, however, say that lightning fires and blazes set by fire experts rarely get out of control. They argue that not permitting fires to burn is actually more dangerous and can lead to a greater risk of **catastrophic** fires. When fires occur after years of **suppression**, flames spread rapidly and furiously through thick and overgrown trees and vegetation. They are not limited to the ground but shoot up trees and cause crown fires.

**DID YOU KNOW?**
The danger of wildfires in an area depends on current and recent weather, the amount of fuel that might burn, and the moisture content of the fuel.

**UNDERSTAND GENRE**
(informational article)
Sometimes authors use facts and opinions to present information.

Identify one fact and one opinion from this part of the article.

Fact: _____

_____

Opinion: _____

_____

**MAKE CONNECTIONS**
Make connections between ideas within a text and real-world events you know about.

Compare wildfires to fires that happen in neighborhoods or cities. How are they the same and different?

Similar:
_____
_____
_____
_____

Different:
_____
_____
_____
_____

**THINK CRITICALLY**
Wildfires can destroy people's homes, harm crops and timber supplies, and spoil landscapes. Why is damage to archeological sites a problem?

_____
_____

**catastrophic** (kat-uh-STROF-ik) relating to a great and sudden event that causes great distress
**suppression** (suh-PRESH-uhn) act of putting an end to; a restraint

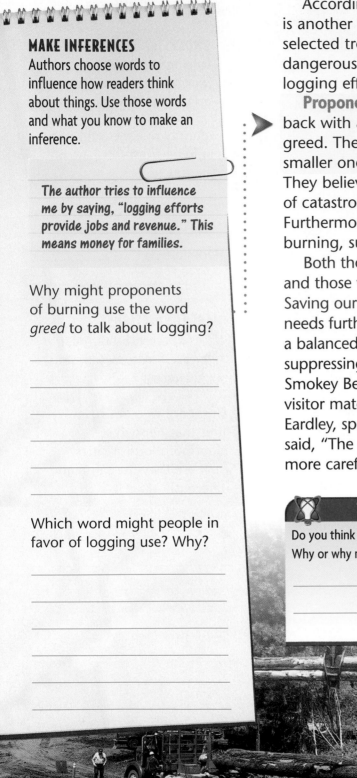

## MAKE INFERENCES

Authors choose words to influence how readers think about things. Use those words and what you know to make an inference.

The author tries to influence me by saying, "logging efforts provide jobs and revenue." This means money for families.

Why might proponents of burning use the word *greed* to talk about logging?

_____

_____

_____

_____

_____

_____

Which word might people in favor of logging use? Why?

_____

_____

_____

_____

_____

**proponents** (pruh-POH-nuntz) people who argue in favor of something

**revenue** (REV-uh-noo) income; money earned

According to some who oppose letting fires burn, there is another solution. Forests can be thinned by cutting down selected trees. They point out that this technique is far less dangerous and costly than playing with fire. In addition, logging efforts provide jobs and **revenue**.

**Proponents** of natural fires and prescribed burning come back with accusations that this suggestion is based on greed. They point out that loggers take large trees, not the smaller ones that need to be removed to reduce fire danger. They believe that logging actually increases the possibility of catastrophic fires because of the debris left behind. Furthermore, logging does not have the helpful effects of burning, such as restoring nutrients to the soil.

Both those who speak for permitting prescribed burning and those who oppose this idea have convincing arguments. Saving our natural wilderness treasures is a complex issue that needs further study. In the meantime, many experts recommend a balanced plan of burning, thinning, and when necessary, suppressing fires. Even ordinary citizens like you are taking Smokey Bear's advice to prevent wildfires. Many parks now offer visitor materials that address the dangers of forest fires. As Randy Eardley, spokesperson for the National Interagency Fire Center, said, "The public has finally gotten more educated about being more careful when they are out recreating and camping."

### THINK CRITICALLY

Do you think economic issues such as jobs should influence decisions about burning? Why or why not?

_____

_____

## Identify Fact and Opinion

The author of this article presents the opinions of people who support prescribed burning and people who oppose it. Facts that support both opinions are also included.

Use the chart below to record supporting evidence from the article. First, write an opinion for each side of the argument. Then write a fact that supports each opinion.

---

**Argument: Is it a good idea to let lightning fires burn and to purposely set other fires in the wilderness?**

| **OPINION** | **OPINION** |
|---|---|
| YES, because | NO, because |
| **SUPPORT** | **SUPPORT** |
| Facts, statistics, and examples: | Facts, statistics, and examples: |

---

### THINK CRITICALLY

Review the opinions and facts recorded in the chart. Which argument do you think is stronger? Why?

_____

_____

_____

Let it Burn?

## Summarize

Summarizing what you learn can help you better remember new information.

Write a brief summary of the arguments for and against controlled wildfires in "Let It Burn?" Use the chart on page 71 to help you.

_____

_____

_____

_____

_____

_____

_____

_____

_____

_____

## Identify the Main Ideas

This article included important points made by proponents and opponents of permitting some natural fires to burn and using prescribed burning. What do you think are two of the most important points made by each side of the debate? Write them below.

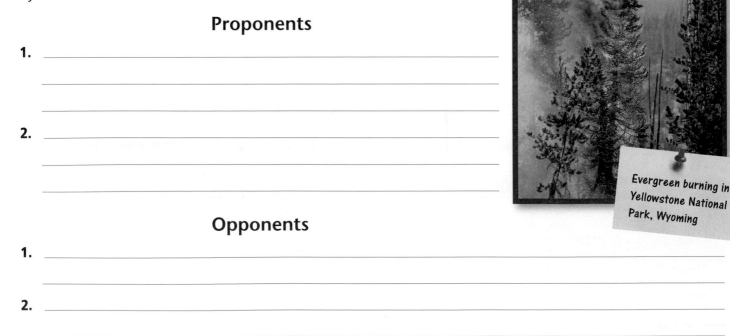

Evergreen burning in Yellowstone National Park, Wyoming

### Proponents

1. _____

_____

2. _____

_____

### Opponents

1. _____

_____

2. _____

_____

## Make Connections

The selections you read were both about forest fires. The author of the informational article included facts. Some of this factual information was also included in the adventure story to make it realistic. Think about what you read and answer the following questions.

**1.** Which two details from the article are included in the adventure story?

_____

_____

_____

**2.** What was an important difference between the fires discussed in "Let It Burn?" and the one in "It's Just My Job"?

_____

_____

**3.** After reading "It's Just My Job," what is your opinion about wilderness firefighting as a career? Use one fact from each selection to support your opinion.

_____

_____

_____

**4.** After reading "Let It Burn?", what do you think might be Marisa's opinion about letting some fires burn? Why?

_____

_____

_____

**5.** Think about another kind of job that involves risk. How is it similar to firefighting?

_____

_____

_____

## Write a Letter

Imagine that you saw Marisa's interview on television. You were so impressed by her story that you decided to write her a letter. In your letter, share your thoughts and feelings about what she does.

_____

_____

_____

_____

_____

_____

_____

_____

_____

_____

**BLACKLINE MASTER** Before you write, use the Blackline Master your teacher will give you to help you plan your letter.

## Plan Your Research

Write three questions you would like to research about forest fires. Use print and online resources to find the answers. Include the information in your letter.

1. _____

_____

2. _____

_____

3. _____

_____

Smokey Bear posters remind people to be careful with fire. This poster is from 1953.

This shameful waste
**WEAKENS AMERICA!**

*Remember—*Only <u>you</u> can
**PREVENT FOREST FIRES!**

## WEB CONNECTION

http://www.OptionsPublishing.com/BestPracticesH

## BRIDGE to Bravery

When Cindy was invited to spend the day sightseeing with her new friend Leya, little did she know that she would be facing one of her biggest fears.

## Recognize Genre

One way authors of **realistic fiction** make their stories believable is by having characters experience the same kinds of feelings that you and people you know have experienced. These feelings are understood through the characters' words, thoughts, and actions.

Plan a realistic fiction story about a character being brave. What would you need to include in a story about bravery? Write four ideas on the lines below.

1. _____

2. _____

3. _____

4. _____

## Connect to the Topic

The main character of this story has a phobia, a strong, unreasonable fear of something. Many people have phobias. List four kinds of phobias that you know about.

1. _____
2. _____
3. _____
4. _____

## Preview and Predict

Reread the introduction and title. Look at the illustrations throughout the story. Write a prediction about what you think will happen in the story.

_____
_____
_____
_____

# READING FICTION

## STRATEGIES

**UNDERSTAND GENRE**
**QUESTION**
**MAKE INFERENCES**
**MAKE CONNECTIONS**

# BRIDGE to Bravery

## UNDERSTAND GENRE

(realistic fiction)
How are Cindy's feelings in this passage like those of a real person?

_____
_____
_____
_____

## QUESTION

Ask yourself questions when you wonder about ideas. Reread or read ahead to find the answer.

Why might Cindy walk across the bridge when she was so afraid?

_____
_____
_____
_____

**Golden Gate** (GOHL-duhn GAYT) narrow waterway between the San Francisco Bay and the Pacific Ocean

**plaque** (PLAHK) tablet inscribed in memory of a person or event

Cindy stood in a parking lot with her new friend, Leya, her friend's grandmother, and about 15 tourists waiting to walk across the Golden Gate Bridge in San Francisco, California. Cindy read the **plaque** on the statue of Joseph Strauss, "The Man Who Built the Bridge."

"I wish you had *not* built the bridge," Cindy grumbled to herself. She frowned as the tour guide intruded upon her thoughts with an enthusiastic, "Welcome to our tour. You are going to learn about this remarkable bridge suspended 240 feet above the **Golden Gate**." Cindy suddenly wished that she had not eaten breakfast. "Why did I get myself into this?" she thought, knowing the answer.

Her family had moved to San Francisco in April. She had been frightened by the idea of transferring to a new school late in the year. The students had been friendly, however, encouraging her to eat lunch with them and walking to classes with her.

Several days ago, a student named Leya had said that her grandmother was coming to the city to do some sightseeing. "Since you are new to the city, why don't you join us?" Leya suggested. Cindy eagerly accepted, not realizing that the day would include a tour of the bridge. Now Cindy had to face her phobia of heights.

**DID YOU KNOW?**

The Golden Gate National Recreation Area, which runs along the Golden Gate, is the largest urban national park in the world.

"You'll want to put on your jackets because the wind is gusty on the bridge," the guide suggested. Cindy's heart sank as she realized another **peril** to worry about…being blown off the bridge!

The guide noticed Cindy's concern, and added, "I promise we won't experience anything like the 70 mile-per-hour wind that blasted the bridge on December 1, 1951. The bridge swayed 24 feet from side to side, but as you can see it's still here!" he joked.

"Oh no," Cindy moaned, wanting desperately to leave. Then she thought, "I can't make Leya and her grandmother miss the tour just because I'm scared. I'll have to get through this somehow." Cindy took a deep breath and followed Leya onto the bridge, noticing with relief that the **pedestrian** walkway was about ten feet wide. She positioned herself on the side away from the water, but her heart was still pounding.

Cindy ignored the guide's talk as she attempted to coach herself through her fear. She discovered that looking straight ahead helped. She could almost imagine she was on a regular street as the noisy traffic bustled by.

## MAKE INFERENCES

Even though the author doesn't directly say it, you can tell what the tour guide is like.

I'll use the information in the story and my own experiences to figure out, or infer, the tour guide's personality.

Use the lines below to explain the tour guide's personality.

_____

_____

_____

_____

Why does the tour guide tell about the 70 mile-per-hour winds?

_____

_____

_____

_____

_____

## THINK CRITICALLY

What other advice would you offer Cindy to help her overcome her fears?

_____

_____

**pedestrian** (puh-DES-tree-uhn) meant for people traveling on foot

**peril** (PEHR-uhl) danger

Describe a picture or souvenir that is important to you and explain why.

_____

_____

_____

_____

_____

_____

Cindy noticed the tour guide pointing at the cables as he explained that the Golden Gate is a **suspension bridge**. "Its cables have a diameter of $36\frac{1}{2}$ inches," he informed the group. Somehow that information was comforting to Cindy. The guide commented that bridges suspended on cables were not a new idea. "Originally, bridge cables were made of vines, and by the 4th century, of braided bamboo."

"Well, I guess things could be worse," Cindy thought. She felt herself relax a little. Her heart had stopped pounding, and her stomach felt better. She chanced glancing down at the water. Realizing that she had not talked with her hosts, she commented to Leya, "The windsurfers down there look like miniature dolls."

Cindy found that she had relaxed enough to listen to the guide's comments. After talking about the **dimensions** of the bridge, he stated, "Maintaining and painting the bridge is a gigantic task, but the paint prevents the bridge from corroding."

"I know what job I *don't* want after I graduate," Cindy joked to Leya. As the girls chuckled, their guide announced, "You have finished your 1.7 mile walk across the Golden Gate Bridge." Cindy couldn't believe that they were on the other side already. Realizing that she had not used the camera hanging around her neck, she turned around and shot a photograph looking up at the towers and cables.

"I am going to hang this picture in my room to remind myself that I am more courageous than I ever realized," Cindy promised herself.

**DID YOU KNOW?**

People have been using rope suspension bridges for more than 2000 years. The Chinese began using iron chains in their suspension bridges during the 500s B.C.E.

**dimensions** (dih-MEN-shuns) width, height, and length measurements of an object

**suspension bridge** (suh-SPEN-shuhn BRIHJ) a bridge in which the roadway is hung from cables anchored at both ends and supported by towers

## Analyze Characters

Readers get to know a character by what the character says, does, and thinks. The character may even change the way he or she feels as a result of the events that take place.

Use the flow chart to write the emotions Cindy experienced and the reasons for them.

| Events | Feelings | Reasons |
|---|---|---|
| Cindy finds out that an outing with a friend includes a bridge tour. | | |
| The tour guide talks about the winds. | | |
| The tour continues. Cindy learns about bridge cables. | | |
| Cindy takes a photograph of the bridge. | | |

### THINK CRITICALLY

In the story, Cindy never tells anyone about her phobia or her worries on the bridge. Reread your flow chart to see how Cindy's feelings change. Will she tell anyone about her phobia now? Why or why not?

_____

_____

_____

## Summarize

When people write letters to friends, they often summarize events that have happened to them. Imagine you are Cindy. Write a brief letter to a friend about the tour of the Golden Gate Bridge. Use the flow chart on page 79 to help you.

_____

_____

_____

_____

_____

_____

_____

_____

## Identify Theme

The theme is the important idea about life that a reader can get from reading a story. Which of the following best expresses the theme of "Bridge to Bravery"? Fill in the circle next to the best answer.

Ⓐ Days with friends are treasured gifts.

Ⓑ A fear of heights is fairly common.

Ⓒ Courage comes from facing fears.

Ⓓ New friends are as good as old friends.

How did learning about the bridge help Cindy learn something about herself?

_____

_____

_____

_____

# Bridges with a History

Think about the last time that you crossed a bridge. Most people take bridges for granted, but some of these structures have interesting stories to tell.

## Recognize Genre

Some **nonfiction articles** share information through a series of comparisons and contrasts. When authors compare and contrast two things, they choose the parts, or features, they want to tell about. Then they decide how to organize their writing so it is clear and interesting. They may use block organization, which first tells about all the features of one thing, and then goes on to tell about all the features of the other. Or, some authors use point-by-point organization. They compare the two things together, feature by feature, or point by point.

Read the headings in the article. How is the information about the two bridges organized?

_____

_____

_____

Aerial view of the
Brooklyn Bridge

## Connect to the Topic

Reread the introduction on this page. Complete the following items to help you think about bridges.

**1.** List three adjectives that describe bridges.

_____

_____

**2.** Name a bridge you have seen in real life, books, or the media. _____

**3.** Write a fact about bridges. _____

_____

## Preview and Predict

Look through the article. Read the headings and study the illustrations. Which questions are most likely to be answered by this article?

(A) How do the Brooklyn Bridge and the Golden Gate Bridge compare?

(B) Were there bridges in ancient times, and how were they built?

(C) How were the Brooklyn Bridge and Golden Gate Bridge built?

(D) Who were the builders of the Brooklyn and Golden Gate Bridges?

**STRATEGIES**

**MAKE INFERENCES**
**MAKE CONNECTIONS**
**UNDERSTAND GENRE**
**VISUALIZE**

# Bridges with a History

**MAKE INFERENCES**
Use details in an article and what you know to make an inference.

Why could the poem also describe the Golden Gate Bridge?

_____
_____
_____
_____
_____
_____
_____
_____
_____
_____

> Against the city's gleaming spires,
> Above the ships that **ply** the stream,
> A bridge of haunting beauty stands—
> Fulfillment of an artist's dream.

These words open a poem by David Steinman about New York's Brooklyn Bridge. They could also describe California's Golden Gate Bridge. These bridges, standing on opposite ends of the United States, are unique but also have much in common.

## The Beginnings of the Brooklyn Bridge

Building a bridge in Brooklyn, a borough of New York City, New York, was suggested in 1802, but the technology had not been invented to create such a structure. Then, in 1867, the state legislature agreed to form a private company to construct a bridge between Brooklyn and Manhattan. The city's growing population had been using ferryboats, which were crowded and dangerous in bad weather, to **commute** across the river. Supposedly, the designer, John Roebling, created the idea for the Brooklyn Bridge on a ferryboat during an ice storm.

## A Builder for the Bridge

Bridge builder John Roebling was asked to design and manage the project. Before construction began, however, tragedy struck. Roebling's foot got caught between two planks on a ferryboat **slip**. His foot was crushed, and Roebling soon died from **tetanus**. Roebling's son, Washington, took over. He, too, suffered misfortune. The younger Roebling developed a crippling disease related to his work on the bridge. He was determined to manage the job from his home, though. His wife, Emily, studied mathematics and engineering and worked with her husband to direct the project.

Portrait of John Augustus Roebling

**commute** (kuh-MYOOT) regular trip between two points

**ply** (PLIE) to travel back and forth across a river, bay, lake, etc.

**slip** (SLIP) docking place for a ship between two piers

**tetanus** (TET-nuhs) serious infectious disease caused by bacteria in the blood from a deep wound

View of the grand display of fireworks on opening night of the Brooklyn Bridge

Photo of the Brooklyn Bridge

## Something to Celebrate

When the Brooklyn Bridge was completed, the opening celebration was held on May 24, 1883. Emily Roebling was the first to ride across the bridge. Pedestrians paid one cent to walk along the raised **promenade**. Eighteen-thousand vehicles crossed for a five-cent toll each.

At the time of its creation, the Brooklyn Bridge was the world's longest suspension bridge. It was also unique in that the wires in its cables, each of which was long enough to stretch from New York to London, were steel rather than iron. Roebling called steel "the material of the future." No doubt, people of the day were worried about the safety of such a long bridge. They must have felt somewhat relieved when circus owner P.T. Barnum paraded 21 elephants across the bridge to show off its strength.

## Planning the Golden Gate Bridge

Three years after construction on the Brooklyn Bridge started in New York in 1869, the Golden Gate Bridge of San Francisco, California was proposed. This bridge would be more than twice as long as the Brooklyn Bridge. It was intended to provide a way, other than ferryboats, to move a growing population between San Francisco and Sausalito. For years, people thought that the project was impossible. Finally, in 1923, with representatives of 21 counties, the Association of Bridging the Gate, **undertook** the task.

### MAKE CONNECTIONS

When you read a selection that sets up comparisons, think about how the information in the first part of the selection compares to the information in the next part.

Write one similarity and one difference between the plan for the Brooklyn Bridge and the plan for the Golden Gate Bridge.

Similarity: _____

_____

_____

Difference: _____

_____

_____

### THINK CRITICALLY

Do you think watching Barnum's elephants march across the Brooklyn Bridge would have convinced you that the bridge was safe? Why or why not?

_____

_____

_____

**promenade** (prahm-uh-NAYD) a space for people to walk, like a path or a sidewalk

**undertook** (un-duhr-TOOK) agreed to do

# Choosing a Builder

Joseph Strauss, a respected builder of more than 400 bridges, was the engineer for the Golden Gate Bridge. Because the project was so huge, many predicted, "Strauss will never build his bridge…." Strauss started the job in 1933, however, and fulfilled his longtime dream of bridging the Golden Gate, faster and less expensively than expected.

Portrait of Joseph B. Strauss, chief engineer of the Golden Gate Bridge in San Francisco

Even though Strauss worked quickly, he was concerned about worker safety. He established strict rules for his builders. This project was the first that required workers to wear hardhats and glare-free goggles. Also, workers were given cream to protect their skin from the wind. They ate special diets to prevent dizziness. The most important **innovation** was a safety net, stretching under the entire bridge. This device saved nineteen workers' lives.

# A Special Event

On May 27, 1937, the opening of the Golden Gate Bridge was celebrated. Two-hundred thousand pedestrians crossed on the ten-foot-wide sidewalks. The following day, President Franklin D. Roosevelt sent a telegram from the White House announcing the completion of the structure. A parade of official cars opened the bridge to automobile traffic.

# Conclusion

Today, millions of people each year drive over both of these **marvels** of human **ingenuity**. Many hardly notice the structures themselves. Others, however, have taken time to capture them in photographs and poems that help us all focus on their usefulness and beauty.

**ingenuity** (in-juh-NOO-ih-tee) cleverness; resourcefulness

**innovation** (in-uh-VAY-shuhn) something new or different

**marvels** (MAR-vuhlz) wonderful or astonishing things

## Identify Details

You learned a lot of information about two bridges by reading "Bridges with a History." Look back through the selection to help you think about how these two structures are alike and different.

Use the chart below to note important information from the article.

|  | Brooklyn Bridge | Golden Gate Bridge |
|---|---|---|
| **Type** |  |  |
| **Purpose** |  |  |
| **Groups who started the project** |  |  |
| **Designers** |  |  |
| **Builders** |  |  |
| **Opening day (Brooklyn Bridge)** |  |  |
| **Opening day (Golden Gate Bridge)** |  |  |

### THINK CRITICALLY

Reread your responses. Think about how the two bridges are alike and different. Then write one main idea that ties together all of the information on your chart.

_____

_____

## Summarize

The author of "Bridges with a History" compared and contrasted two bridges. Review what you learned by writing side-by-side summaries. Use the chart on page 85 to help you.

| **Brooklyn Bridge** | **Golden Gate Bridge** |
| --- | --- |
| | |

## Identify Details

The author introduced this article by saying that the Brooklyn and Golden Gate Bridges have much in common. What are three details that support this main idea?

1. _____

2. _____

3. _____

## Make Connections

Think about the two selections you have just read. Think about how the pieces are connected. Certain parts of "Bridge to Bravery" might have helped you understand "Bridges with a History." Think about what you learned from the nonfiction piece that improved your understanding of the fiction selection. Answer the following questions.

**1.** If the author had used the Brooklyn Bridge as the setting for "Bridge to Bravery," which two details would have to be changed?

- _____

- _____

**2.** If Cindy had known more about Joseph Strauss and the building of the Golden Gate Bridge, she might have felt more confident. Which two facts from "Bridges with a History" might have comforted Cindy?

- _____

- _____

**3.** Think about a bridge that is familiar to you. What is one similarity and one difference between that bridge and the ones you have read about?

**Similarity:** _____

_____

_____

**Difference:** _____

_____

_____

## Plan a Brochure

You read about a tour of the Golden Gate Bridge in "Bridge to Bravery." Now think about a tour of the Brooklyn Bridge. What would you say in a brochure for a tour of the bridge? Think about what you learned about the bridge. Make some notes below about what you would include in the brochure.

_____

_____

_____

_____

_____

_____

_____

_____

 Before you write, use the Blackline Master your teacher will give you to plan your brochure.

Many people walk across the Brooklyn Bridge to get a view of the New York City skyline.

## Plan Your Research

Recall what you read about the Brooklyn Bridge. Use print and online resources to learn more. Write three questions you have about the bridge on the lines below.

1. _____

_____

2. _____

_____

3. _____

_____

### WEB CONNECTION

http://www.OptionsPublishing.com/BestPracticesH

It is December 1814, and the United States is at war with Great Britain. The pirate
Lafitte (lah-FEET) needs information about General Jackson. He thinks he can help
the general save New Orleans. Can Jean-Pierre help him?

## Recognize Genre

**Fiction** stories are made up by an author.
**Historical fiction** is a story that takes place in
the past. The setting might be ancient Egypt or the
United States during the 1940s. Some characters and
events may be taken from history. Others
are drawn from the author's imagination.
The author usually
makes up the
dialogue.

Decide whether each statement about historical
fiction is true or false. Circle **T** or **F**.

**T**  **F**  In historical fiction, historical figures
speak only words they actually said.

**T**  **F**  In historical fiction, the plot is made up
by the author.

Write one true statement and one false statement
about historical fiction.

_____

_____

_____

## Connect to the Topic

Reread the above introduction to "Jean-Pierre
and the Pirates." Ask yourself: *What do I know
about New Orleans?* Fill in the bubble next to two
statements that you think are true.

(A) Pirates attack ships in New Orleans.

(B) The British attacked New Orleans during the
War of 1812.

(C) New Orleans is in France.

(D) New Orleans is a city near water.

## Preview and Predict

Take a quick look at the story. Think about the title,
illustrations, and topic. Use the information to make
a prediction. What do you think you will read about
in "Jean-Pierre and the Pirates"?

_____

_____

_____

_____

_____

**STRATEGIES**

MAKE CONNECTIONS
MAKE INFERENCES
UNDERSTAND GENRE
QUESTION

**MAKE CONNECTIONS**

Compare your experiences and feelings to those of a character.

When have you felt grown up and independent?

**MAKE INFERENCES**

Use clues and what you know to figure out what the text means.

Why might the two men want to meet with General Jackson?

"Jean-Pierre, run over to the *Amité* and ask Captain Rampal when he will unload his cargo. Tell him the storerooms are empty."

"Yes, Papa." Jean-Pierre was happy to go. He was fourteen and loved being out on the docks among the ships and sailors from all over the world. He felt lucky to live in a great port city like New Orleans. Life was even better since France sold the city and all of the Louisiana Territory to the United States. Even if his new country was at war and enemy ships were anchored a hundred miles down the Mississippi River, Jean-Pierre was not worried.

Lost in thought, he dashed around a corner and found himself face to face with two **imposing** strangers. The first was tall and elegantly dressed. A sword hung at his side. His companion was a short, thickset man with a **slovenly** appearance.

"Ho, what have we here, Dominique?" the taller man remarked. "This lad might serve our purposes very well. What is your name, boy?"

"Jean-Pierre, sir."

"Well, Jean-Pierre, what do you know about General Andrew Jackson, who has come to save our fair city from the British? Do you know where he is to be found?"

"I know where his headquarters are, sir."

"Ah, excellent. My brother and I seek a meeting with General Jackson, but he is . . . **reluctant** to see us. So we plan to meet him accidentally. To do that, we need to know his habits—when he goes out for refreshment, where he goes. Do you understand?"

**DID YOU KNOW?**

In 1803, the United States bought New Orleans as part of the Louisiana Purchase. The sale covered 828,000 square miles and cost only 3¢ an acre!

**imposing** (im-POHZ-ing) making a strong impression

**reluctant** (rih-LUK-tunt) unwilling to do something

**slovenly** (SLUV-uhn-lee) untidy

"Y-y-yes, sir."

"Very well, bring us this information here tomorrow at this same hour," commanded the tall stranger. "There will be a reward for you, as well as the knowledge that you have done your patriotic duty."

In an instant, they were gone. Jean-Pierre quickly finished the errand for his father and headed for Royal Street, where General Jackson had his headquarters. That was the easy part, but how could he find out about the general's habits?

Just then Jean-Pierre spotted an inn directly across the street from the headquarters. A young boy was leading a horse around the back to the barn. Jean-Pierre caught up with him and began to **ply** him with questions: Did he ever see General Jackson? Did Jackson dine at the inn? When?

"Sure, I see the general," the boy said. "Doesn't Old Hickory come here directly at noon every day for his bowl of boiled rice? You know, the general's got a bad stomach. Can't eat a thing but boiled rice."

Just then, a soldier came around the corner. The boy with the horse blurted out, "Corporal Jones, sir, this young man's been asking about Old Hickory. Wants to know when he eats and all."

"Is that right? Well now, lad, you wouldn't be a British spy, would you?" He grabbed Jean-Pierre roughly by the arm. "I think we'd better ask *you* some questions."

Panicked, Jean-Pierre twisted his arm and pulled away. In a flash, he was out in the street with the corporal right behind him.

## THINK CRITICALLY

The boy suggests to the soldier that Jean-Pierre is asking suspicious questions. Why do you think the boy told the soldier about Jean-Pierre?

_____

_____

_____

### UNDERSTAND GENRE

(historical fiction)
Authors of historical fiction usually do research to make their description of a time period correct. For example, Andrew Jackson's headquarters really were on Royal Street. However, authors also make up details in a story.

Write one detail about Jackson that you think is true and one you think is made-up.

True: _____

_____

_____

Made-up: _____

_____

_____

Write a detail that indicates this story is set in the past.

_____

_____

_____

**ply** (PLIE) to pester, ask again and again

When you are not sure about an event, a word, or an idea, stop reading and ask yourself some questions. Reread, read ahead, or use a dictionary to help you find answers.

*What is the difference between a pirate and a privateer? I read the dictionary below to make things clear.*

If the general knows the difference between a pirate and a privateer, which does he think Lafitte is?

_____

_____

_____

_____

How can you tell?

_____

_____

_____

_____

Turning the corner, Jean-Pierre almost ran into another soldier.

"Grab him," yelled the corporal, but Jean-Pierre sprinted away. The two soldiers chased the boy for a few blocks and then gave up. Panting, Jean-Pierre arrived at his father's office. To his amazement, there were the two men he had met just a few hours earlier.

His father told him, "Jean-Pierre, you have the honor to meet Jean Lafitte (lah-FEET), the most famous **privateer** in America, and his brother Dominique. They want to help General Jackson defend New Orleans from the British."

"The general needs men and weapons. I can provide them, but Jackson doesn't want our help. He thinks we are **pirates**," laughed the tall one, the one his father called Lafitte. "But he doesn't understand the difference between a pirate and a privateer."

"I can take you to the general, sir," stated Jean-Pierre, proudly.

"Then we are off."

As Jean-Pierre's father stared in amazement, his son led the two men off toward Royal Street. They arrived just before noon and stood casually talking in the street. Soon a tall, slim man with steely-blue eyes emerged from a door and strode across the street. Lafitte was at his side in an instant.

"A word, I beg you, General. Permit me to introduce myself."

Jean-Pierre didn't hear the rest, but he saw Old Hickory's face slowly turn from a **stony** stare to a warm smile, and he knew that New Orleans had nothing to fear from the British.

## THINK CRITICALLY

Imagine you are Jean Lafitte. What would you have said to make General Jackson smile?

_____

_____

_____

**pirates** (PIE-ritz) people who attack and rob ships at sea

**privateer** (prie-vuh-TEER) captain and crew of a privately owned ship hired by a country at war to seize enemy ships, especially merchant ships

**stony** (STOH-nee) cold; hard; uninterested

Jean-Pierre *and the* PiraTes

## Identify Story Elements

The plot of a story is the series of events that take you from beginning to end. What usually makes the plot interesting is the main character's attempt to solve one or more problems. Think about the problem that Jean-Pierre faces in "Jean-Pierre and the Pirates" and the two important events that happen to him in the story. Then complete the story map.

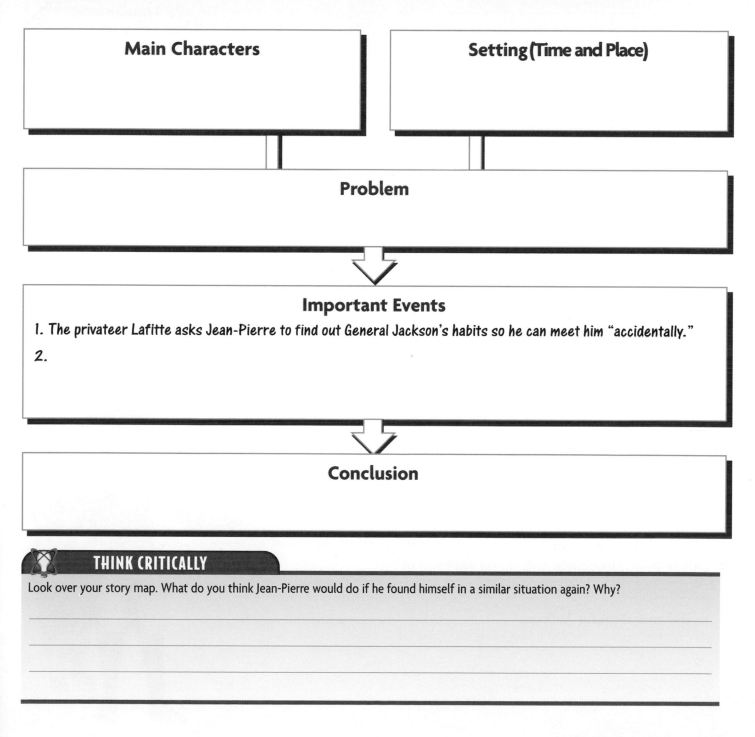

**Main Characters**

**Setting (Time and Place)**

**Problem**

**Important Events**

1. The privateer Lafitte asks Jean-Pierre to find out General Jackson's habits so he can meet him "accidentally."

2.

**Conclusion**

**THINK CRITICALLY**

Look over your story map. What do you think Jean-Pierre would do if he found himself in a similar situation again? Why?

_____

_____

_____

## Summarize

Summarizing, telling the key elements of a story, is a good way to review what you have read and make sure you remember the most important points.

Briefly summarize what happened in "Jean-Pierre and the Pirates." You can use the story map on page 93 to help you.

_____

_____

_____

_____

_____

_____

_____

_____

> I should mention the setting and the main character, the problem the main character faces, and how it is solved.

## Identify Plot

When you tell what happens in a story, focus on the important events. Complete each sentence below so that it states an important event from "Jean-Pierre and the Pirates."

**1.** Jean-Pierre agrees to help _____

by _____ .

**2.** Jean-Pierre finds out _____

by _____ .

**3.** General Jackson does not want to meet Lafitte because

_____

_____ .

**4.** Lafitte hopes to convince General Jackson to _____

_____ .

**5.** In the end, General Jackson _____

_____ .

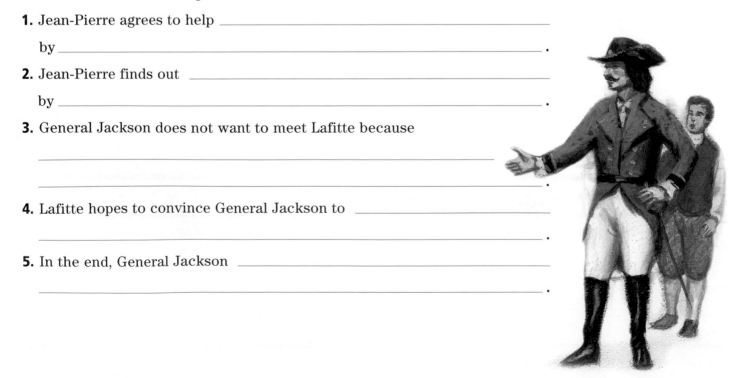

# The Last Battle

In 1814, the British decided to attack New Orleans. Things looked bad for America. Find out what happened at the last battle ever fought between the United States and Great Britain. Did Lafitte live up to his promise and help General Jackson win?

## Recognize Genre

**Nonfiction** is different from fiction because it provides facts about real people, places, and events. An **informational article** is a type of nonfiction that might be found in a newspaper or magazine. It may contain information about science, history, current events, or any other aspect of the real world.

Informational articles often have photos or illustrations that help you understand the content of the article. Captions explain what is being shown. Look quickly through the article "The Last Battle." Then fill in the bubble beside each type of visual you find.

(A) portrait of an historical figure

(B) chart of battle casualties

(C) comparison chart of two armies

(D) map

(E) photographs

(F) artist's painting of a real event

Which visual would be the most helpful for understanding where the battle occurred? Why?

_____

_____

_____

## Connect to the Topic

Reread the introduction to "The Last Battle" on this page. Recall what you learned about Jean Lafitte and Andrew Jackson in "Jean-Pierre and the Pirates." Write two facts you know about Jean Lafitte or Andrew Jackson.

1. _____

_____

_____

2. _____

_____

_____

## Preview and Predict

Preview the article by looking at the three section headings. Write one thing you think you will learn about in each section.

1. _____

_____

2. _____

_____

3. _____

**QUESTIONS**

As you read nonfiction, ask questions about any facts or ideas you are unsure of.

Why would Franklin say "...the War of Independence is still to be fought"?

_____

_____

_____

_____

Write another question you have so far. Then underline the answer.

_____

_____

_____

_____

_____

_____

**ragtag** (RAG-tag) messy; disorganized

**stamina** (STAM-uh-nuh) energy; determination; endurance

**stern** (STURN) strict or harsh; not gentle

# The Last Battle

## The Second War for Independence

Portrait of Major General Andrew Jackson

In 1781, a **ragtag** army of American colonists defeated the mightiest country in the world, and the American Revolution against Britain ended. However, the end of the war wasn't the end of America's conflicts with Britain. As Benjamin Franklin put it, "The War of the Revolution has been won, but the War of Independence is still to be fought."

For one thing, Britain was soon involved in a war with Napoleon's France. To keep their warships fully manned, British captains often stopped American merchant ships and forced the sailors into serving on their ships. The practice was called impressment, and Americans greatly resented it. They also resented the fact that Britain aided Native Americans who were resisting the westward expansion of the United States.

Finally, the United States government lost patience. On June 18, 1812, Congress declared war on Britain. For the next two years, British and American armies fought several battles in the northern and western United States with no clear-cut victory for either side.

In April of 1814, Napoleon surrendered, leaving Britain free to send its European troops to America. With more soldiers, the British decided to move the war into the South. The lively and valuable port of New Orleans was their choice for a battleground. The American military leader the British had to face was Major General Andrew Jackson, better known as Old Hickory because of his **stern** personality and his **stamina**.

# Preparations for Battle

Jackson and some of his troops arrived in New Orleans in the late fall of 1814. He immediately went to work organizing citizen groups for the defense of the city, but he was troubled by the lack of weapons. Help soon came from Jean Lafitte, whose men were experienced fighters familiar with the swamps and **bayous** around New Orleans. Lafitte also provided guns and ammunition, which Jackson badly needed.

In the meantime, the British were making their own plans, after having been **rebuffed** by Lafitte when they offered to pay for his help. They had six possible attack routes. Sailing one hundred miles up the Mississippi River from the Gulf of Mexico, they would have had to face the guns of Fort St. Philip. Instead, they anchored their ships in the Gulf of Mexico and had sailors row thousands of men across Lake Borgne to get closer to the city. After enduring a full week of freezing rain without shelter, a thousand of these men were unfit for battle and had to return to the ships.

It looked as if luck was on the side of the British, however, when they discovered an unguarded bayou that led to the Villeré Plantation. On December 23rd, the British encamped on the plantation to rest and to have their first hot meal in a week. It was a big mistake.

## DID YOU KNOW?

The British offered Jean Lafitte $30,000 to help their side. Instead, he aided the United States, and President Madison pardoned Lafitte's earlier illegal activities.

**MAKE CONNECTIONS**
Connect new information with something you already know.

Describe a swamp area you've seen or read about.

_____

_____

_____

**UNDERSTAND GENRE**
(informational article)
Informational articles often contain visual aids to help readers understand the text.

Which locations in the article can be found on the map?

_____

_____

What other information does the map give you?

_____

_____

_____

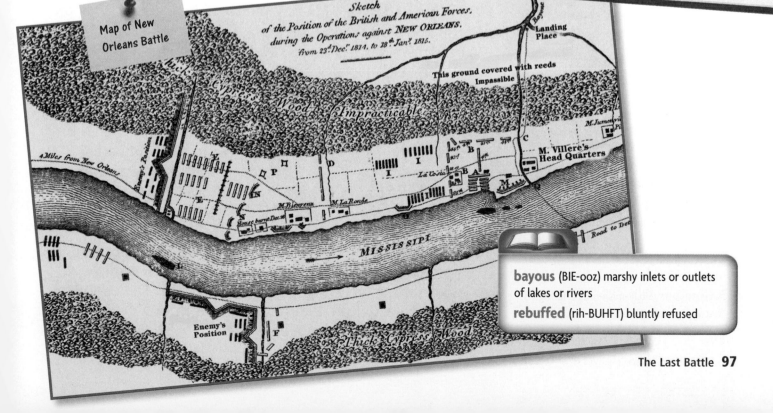

Map of New Orleans Battle

Sketch of the Position of the British and American Forces, during the Operations against NEW ORLEANS, from 23rd Dec.r 1814, to 18th Jan.y 1815.

**bayous** (BIE-ooz) marshy inlets or outlets of lakes or rivers
**rebuffed** (rih-BUHFT) bluntly refused

The Last Battle **97**

General Andrew Jackson rides the white horse in this famous painting of the Battle of New Orleans.

**VISUALIZE**
Authors include descriptions to help you imagine a place.

When I read about the barricade, I had a clear picture of what it looked like and what was happening.

What does the barricade look like to you, and what do you "see" happening?

_____

_____

_____

_____

_____

_____

Which words does the author use to describe the battlefield? Circle them.

barricade (BEHR-uh-cayd) a pile of things built up to block a road or entrance

battalions (buh-TAL-yuns) large groups of soldiers

militia (muh-LISH-uh) citizen army called up in times of emergency

skirmishes (SKUR-mish-uhz) brief fights between small groups

# On the Battlefield

Jackson was shocked to discover that the British were within ten miles of New Orleans. He gathered his forces, regular army soldiers, **militia** groups from several states, two **battalions** of free African Americans, and a band of Chocktaw Indians, and went on the offensive. At 8:00 P.M. on December 23, Lafitte's forces surprised the exhausted British, but neither side emerged the winner.

The next day, Jackson and his troops set up their position a few miles west of the British. They built a **barricade** of logs, earth, and cotton bales. Lafitte's group operated the naval guns from the top of the barricade. Three-quarters of a mile long, the line was anchored at one end by a swamp and at the other end by the Mississippi River. There was no way the British could go around it.

After several small **skirmishes**, the British decided to attack at daybreak on January 8. Advancing across a flat, muddy field directly at the American line, not one British soldier made it over the barricade. By 8:30 A.M. the British had surrendered. Over two thousand British soldiers were dead or wounded, including three generals. American casualties numbered under one hundred. The Battle of New Orleans was over. Outnumbered 8,000 to 4,000, Old Hickory led the Americans to victory.

As for the War of 1812, on February 14, 1815, a ship brought the news from Europe that American and British representatives had signed a peace treaty on December 24, the day Jackson was building his fortified line. The two-week Battle of New Orleans was fought between two nations that were at peace and have been ever since.

*The* **Last Battle**

## Identify Cause and Effect

"The Last Battle" includes several causes and effects related to the Battle of New Orleans. A cause is the reason why something happens. An effect is what happens as a result of the cause.

The chart below lists causes and effects. For each cause given, fill in an effect. For each effect given, fill in a cause.

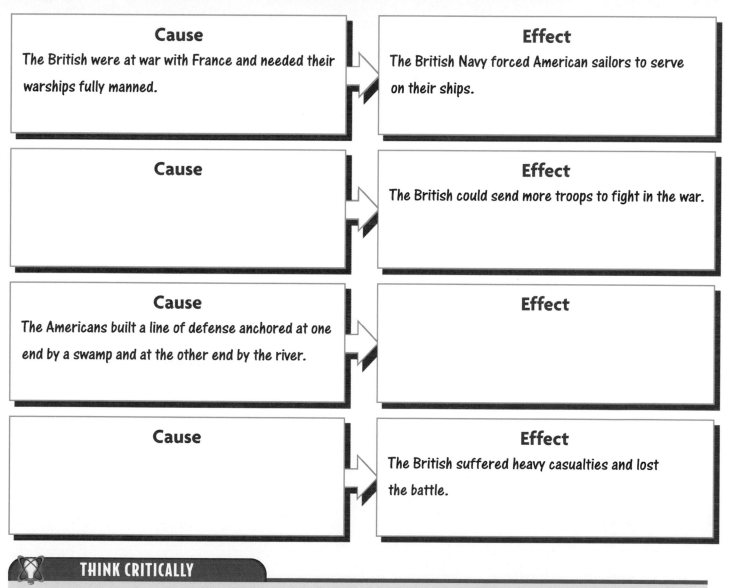

| **Cause** | **Effect** |
|---|---|
| The British were at war with France and needed their warships fully manned. | The British Navy forced American sailors to serve on their ships. |
| **Cause** | **Effect** |
| | The British could send more troops to fight in the war. |
| **Cause** | **Effect** |
| The Americans built a line of defense anchored at one end by a swamp and at the other end by the river. | |
| **Cause** | **Effect** |
| | The British suffered heavy casualties and lost the battle. |

### ⚛ THINK CRITICALLY

The United States won the Battle of New Orleans. What effect do you think that had on U.S. relations with Britain? Explain your answer.

_____

_____

## Summarize

On tests, you may be asked to summarize the key points of an informational article. The key points of an historical event should be summarized in chronological order, the order in which events happened.

Summarize "The Last Battle." Include the most important causes and effects from the chart on page 99.

> I should start by writing the name of the war and which two countries fought in it. Then I should name the battle and write about the most important events.

_____

_____

_____

_____

_____

_____

_____

_____

## Identify the Main Ideas

The headings in an article can help you figure out the main ideas. For each heading, ask yourself: *What is the most important idea from this section?*

Below are the three headings from "The Last Battle." Write the most important idea under each one.

> I will have to restate the most important idea from each section in my own words.

**1.** The Second War for Independence _____

_____

_____.

**2.** Preparations for Battle _____

_____

_____.

**3.** On the Battlefield _____

_____

_____.

# Make Connections

What you read will make more sense to you if you connect it to other selections you have read, your own experiences, and the world around you. Answer the following questions.

**1.** What did you learn about Jean Lafitte and Andrew Jackson in "Jean-Pierre and the Pirates" that added to your understanding of "The Last Battle"?

_____

_____

_____

_____

**2.** Think about what you read in both selections. Why was General Jackson initially unwilling to meet with Jean Lafitte?

_____

_____

_____

_____

**3.** Communication during the War of 1812 was different than today. News of peace between the two countries came after the war had been fought. Describe changes that have occurred in how people communicate since then.

**People used to communicate by** _____

_____ .

**Now, they communicate by** _____

_____ .

**4.** Use what you learned in both selections to explain why you think Jean Lafitte helped the Americans instead of the British.

_____

_____

_____

# Write a News Story

A news story should answer the questions *Who?, What?, When?, Where?, Why?,* and *How?* Imagine you are a reporter on assignment in New Orleans at the time of the Battle of New Orleans. Write a news story about the battle that answers these questions. Be sure to give your story an interesting headline.

_____

_____

_____

_____

_____

_____

_____

_____

_____

_____

**BLACKLINE MASTER** Before you write, use the Blackline Master your teacher will give you to plan your news story.

# Plan Your Research

What else would you like to know about the Battle of New Orleans, the War of 1812, or Jean Lafitte? Pick a topic. Write three questions and then use print and online resources to find the answers.

Topic: _____

Questions:

1. _____

2. _____

3. _____

## ⬅ WEB CONNECTION

http://www.OptionsPublishing.com/BestPracticesH

Welcome aboard the International Space Station, where three astronauts are growing plants in zero gravity. In this story, the experiment takes an interesting twist when one astronaut decides to talk to the plants.

## Recognize Genre

**Fictional** stories are made up by authors. Every work of fiction has a setting, characters, and a plot. **Realistic fiction** has believable characters doing believable things in a setting that may or may not exist. In realistic fiction, the details are true-to-life even though the story is made up.

"Space Garden" is a realistic story about working in space. Place a check next to each realistic detail you might find in the story.

| Characters: | a Martian man |
| | a Spanish-speaking man |
| **Setting:** | a space station |
| | the sun |
| **Events:** | plants talk to people |
| | a computer waters plants |

Describe a character and an event that could appear in a realistic story.

Character: _____

Event: _____

_____

## Connect to the Topic

Reread the above introduction to "Space Garden." Ask yourself: *What do I know about astronauts? What do I know about working in space?* Circle **T** true or **F** for false next to each statement.

**T** **F** Astronauts must train a long time for living and working in space.

**T** **F** In space, astronauts experience weightlessness.

**T** **F** Astronauts don't eat or drink while living in space.

## Preview and Predict

Preview the story. Think about the title and illustrations. Make predictions about what you will read in "Space Garden."

**Who** are the characters? _____

_____

**Where** does the action take place? _____

_____

**What** are the characters doing? _____

_____

## STRATEGIES

**MAKE PREDICTIONS**
**VISUALIZE**
**MAKE INFERENCES**
**QUESTION**
**UNDERSTAND GENRE**

Space Garden

### MAKE PREDICTIONS

Use events that have happened in a story so far to predict what might happen next.

What might happen when Jorge goes to tend to the plants?

### VISUALIZE

Picture what the setting looks like. Imagining it helps you understand and enjoy the story.

How do you imagine the space station as Jorge moves around inside it?

**nutrients** (NOO-tree-uhntz) nourishing substances in food

**zero gravity** (ZEER-oh GRAV-ih-tee) the condition of being weightless

Looking out the window, Jorge thought, "I am the luckiest guy on Earth to be able to see what I am seeing." Then he chuckled to himself. "Of course, I'm not *on* Earth. If I were, I wouldn't have this view." Again, he looked out the window of the International Space Station and saw his home planet drifting slowly by 220 miles away.

There was time for daydreaming on the space station, but there was also plenty of work to do. Now Jorge had to tend to his mission's main experiment: the space garden, as he and the other two crew members called it.

He floated toward the Laboratory Module where the experimental garden was growing. Floating around the space station in **zero gravity** was a fun part of the job.

When Jorge reached the Laboratory Module, Pilot Steve Wong and Commander Elya Gordeeva were already checking out one of the experiments.

"Jorge, what are you up to?" asked Elya.

"I have to go tend to my plants," he responded.

Actually, most of the work had been done back on Earth. Scientists had developed the growth chamber, a completely enclosed tray where the temperature, humidity, light, and delivery of water and **nutrients** to the plants were controlled by a computer. They had planted seeds in a rooting material and attached the seed tray to the growth chamber. All Jorge had to do was check the plants now and then and report what he saw to the lab.

**DID YOU KNOW?**

The first woman in space was Valentina Tereshkova from the Soviet Union, in 1963.

Jorge removed the growth chamber from the rack and peered at it. He could see small green shoots. It looked like most of the seeds had **germinated**. Without realizing what he was doing, Jorge began to talk to the plants. He introduced himself and offered encouraging words.

"What did you say, Jorge?" Steve asked as he floated over.

"I'm not talking to *you*, Steve. Just giving the *Arabidopsis* (air-uh-bih-DOP-sis) some encouragement."

"Who?"

"*Arabidopsis!* The plants we're growing. They're related to cabbages and radishes. The scientists say if we can grow plants that produce seeds in **microgravity**, future space missions could grow their own fresh vegetables."

"Uh-huh," nodded Steve. "And did the scientists tell you to talk to the plants?"

"Well, not exactly. My mom read this book once. It said that if you talk to your houseplants, they'll grow better. So I thought it couldn't hurt to give the *Arabidopsis* a few friendly words."

"Elya," Steve called. "This guy is talking to the plants. Do you think we should notify the doctor?"

Elya laughed. "I don't think there's anything wrong with Jorge. But if those plants get too big, the lab's not going to be happy. They specifically chose a plant species that wouldn't grow too large."

"Laugh all you want," grinned Jorge. "But I'm planning to take some prize-winning Arabidopsis back to Earth. A few years from now, when you're orbiting Mars and eating fresh greens, you just remember it was Jorge Mendes who encouraged their great-grandmother to produce good seeds."

**DID YOU KNOW?**

Fresh vegetables would be a treat for astronauts. Much of their food is dehydrated so it will take up less space and it won't spoil.

**MAKE INFERENCES**

Use details in a story and what you know to make an inference.

Why might it be important for future space missions to grow their own vegetables?

_____

_____

_____

_____

_____

_____

**QUESTION**

When you come to a part of the story that you're not sure of, stop reading and ask yourself questions. Reread or read on to help clear things up.

What do you think Jorge means when he says, ". . . It was Jorge who encouraged their great-grandmother to produce good seeds"?

_____

_____

_____

_____

**germinated** (JUR-muh-nay-tid) started to grow

**microgravity** (MY-kroh GRAV-ih-tee) near weightlessness caused by slight gravity when an object orbits Earth

(realistic fiction)
When you read realistic fiction, look at the details that make the setting, characters, and plot believable.

Write one detail that makes Steve a realistic character.

_____

_____

_____

In realistic fiction, authors sometimes include familiar details. These details make the story seem as if it could really happen.

What details about life on the space station seem real because they are so familiar?

1. _____

_____

2. _____

_____

That night, Jorge was listening to music through his headphones. Elya was emailing her family in Russia. Steve floated up to her when Jorge wasn't looking.

"Elya, I've got a great idea for a joke to play on Jorge. We'll make an audio recording of me talking to him as if I'm one of the plants. Then we'll hide the recorder near the plants. The next time he works there, one of us will sneak over and push the PLAY button."

"What will you say in the recording?" asked Elya.

"Oh, I'll tell him how glad all of us plants are that he is taking such good care of us."

"You think he will believe that?" asked Elya.

"Not really, but it'll be a good laugh," chuckled Steve.

"OK, let's do it!" they both agreed.

A few weeks later, Jorge had to refill the nutrient container for the plant chamber. As he worked, he muttered to the plants. Steve floated over.

Suddenly, Jorge heard a low voice. But Steve's lips weren't moving.

"Did you hear that?" Jorge asked.

"I didn't hear anything," Steve replied. "Did you hear anything, Elya?"

"**Nyet**," she answered.

Jorge tried his best to control the grin that was breaking out on his face. "I could swear the plants were talking back to me. They said they're glad I'm taking care of them."

"Really?" asked Steve, trying to hide his own grin.

"Yes," Jorge laughed. "Funny thing is, I talk to them in Spanish, but they're answering in English."

With that, the astronauts had a good laugh as they celebrated the progress of their prized cargo.

## THINK CRITICALLY

These astronauts will be living together in a small space for some time. Do you think it's a good idea for them to play jokes on each other? Why or why not?

_____

_____

_____

nyet (NYET) Russian word for *no*

## Analyze Characters

In "Space Garden," you get to know the characters through what they think, say, and do. The author tells you about Jorge through his actions. Complete the character web below. For each trait that you identify, give an example of a thought, phrase, or action that demonstrates that trait.

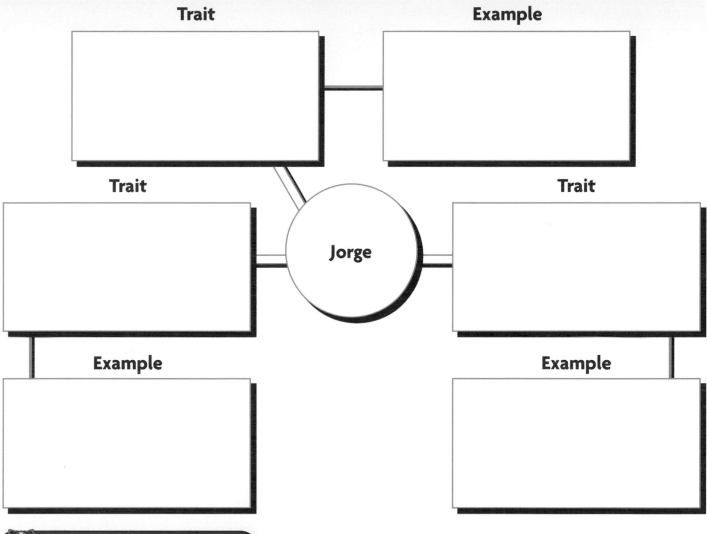

**Trait**

**Example**

**Trait**

Jorge

**Trait**

**Example**

**Example**

### THINK CRITICALLY

Review the web. How does Jorge's personality affect the story's ending? To help you answer this question, think about how the ending might change if Jorge had different traits.

## Summarize

In the summary of a story, it's important to include the setting (where and when), main characters (who), and the plot (what happens). Write a summary of "Space Garden" and include these story elements.

_____

_____

_____

_____

_____

_____

_____

_____

## Identify Details

Stories are realistic when they contain some factual details.

Read the sentences below. Fill in the bubble next to the three factual details that are included in "Space Garden."

(A) Astronauts on the space station come from different countries.

(B) Most people think gardening is fun and relaxing.

(C) It helps to have a sense of humor when you spend a long time in a small space with other people.

(D) Astronauts can listen to music and write e-mails while they are in space.

(E) Astronauts on a long space journey must get along with one another.

(F) Astronauts can see Earth from 220 miles away.

Look through the story for another fact. Write it below.

_____

_____

_____

# FOR A ROBOTIC MOON BASE

Exploring outer space has been a job for some people and machines for many years. Could people continue to explore areas far beyond the moon, or can machines take over some jobs?

## Recognize Genre

A **persuasive essay** is a kind of nonfiction that contains not only facts but also the author's opinions about a topic. In a persuasive essay, the author tries to convince readers to agree with his or her opinions by presenting a strong argument. The argument may reach out to readers' feelings, but it also contains facts that support the author's opinions.

Look through the article. Write two features that you see in this persuasive essay that you would also see in other nonfiction.

_____

_____

How might these features help you understand the topic of the selection?

_____

_____

## Connect to the Topic

Reread the introduction to "For a Robotic Moon Base." Think about the story "Space Garden." Write two things you know about exploration in outer space.

**1.** _____

_____

**2.** _____

_____

## Preview and Predict

Scan the essay. Look at the title, headings, and photographs. Then make a prediction. What is one argument that the author might use to support his or her opinion?

_____

_____

The launching of a space shuttle

**STRATEGIES**

**MAKE PREDICTIONS**
**QUESTION**
**DRAW CONCLUSIONS**

**FOR A ROBOTIC MOON BASE**

Since 1959, Antarctica has been set aside as a scientific **preserve**. Every year, more than 4,000 scientists from around the world work at **permanent** research stations there. Someday, people may establish another permanent **outpost**, this time in a place that we have all seen but which is far from home. Perhaps this base will be on the moon.

## What Model Should Be Used?

Antarctica should be our model for a moon base. At first, individual countries claimed as their own the parts of Antarctica that they explored. However, in an example of wise **collaboration**, the countries later agreed in 1959 that there would be no more individual claims.

Antarctica became a continent without countries. It is open to all countries for scientific work, but no country may take its resources, build a military base, or put weapons there. Our moon base should be similar. It should be a cooperative effort of all the people of Earth. All countries should be given the right to join if they wish to. The moon should be set aside as a preserve. No country should be allowed to claim any part of it. Like Antarctica, the moon should be open to all countries for peaceful work.

**MAKE PREDICTIONS**
Use the information you have read so far to make a prediction about the topic.

What kind of peaceful work might the author argue the moon base should be used for? Explain your answer.

_____

_____

_____

_____

_____

_____

_____

_____

The Concordia Station in Antarctica is being used to train crews for missions to other planets.

**collaboration** (kuh-lab-uh-RAY-shun) the act of working together; cooperation

**outpost** (OWT-post) distant settlement; colony

**permanent** (PUR-muh-nunt) lasting for a long time

**preserve** (prih-ZERV) an area set aside for study and protection

A computer-generated model of a moon base that would shelter a small crew of astronauts

## For Which Purposes?

A base on the moon should be used for scientific study. A permanent base would offer great opportunities for scientists who study outer space. For one thing, we could build telescopes there that would be much more powerful than telescopes that are put into orbit. A telescope built on the moon could be more complex because it would not have to survive a space launch. Any fragile parts would not be affected by movement.

In addition, a moon base would become the ideal place for further space exploration. Because the moon's gravity is much weaker than Earth's gravity, space vehicles launched from the moon could be smaller, lighter, and more **cost-effective** than those launched from Earth.

The moon could become the first stepping stone in our visits to other planets. From the moon, we would make the step to Mars, from Mars to Venus, and so on. A permanent moon base would allow scientists to explore without being wasteful of money and time.

## Why Permanent?

Today, our space programs are costly. Some would even say the equipment is **expendable**. We use a rocket for a single trip and then **dispose** of it. We put a satellite or space station into orbit and then allow it to burn on re-entry. These practices are wasteful. In the long run, permanent equipment is cheaper than temporary equipment. A permanent base would make better use of our resources, our energies, and our money. A permanent base can grow, expand, and improve over time.

**DID YOU KNOW?**

If you weigh 120 pounds on Earth, you would weigh only 20 pounds on the moon.

**QUESTION**

When you're not sure of something, stop reading and ask yourself a question. Reread or read ahead to find the answer.

Why could a telescope built on the moon be more complex? I reread and figured out that it could have delicate parts that won't break because it won't be launched.

Write one question you have about what you've read so far.

_____

_____

_____

Now write the answer to your question.

_____

_____

_____

_____

**cost-effective** (cawst-ih-FEHK-tihv) to make the best use of money

**dispose** (dih-SPOHZ) to get rid of or throw out

**expendable** (ek-SPEN-duh-buhl) not meant to be saved or re-used

# Why Robots?

While some humans would of course be necessary to run the moon base, robots may be the best way to explore space. The cost of supporting people in space—getting them there safely, keeping them alive while they are there, and returning them to Earth safely—is so high that it leaves little money for running scientific investigations.

Machines are far easier to send through space than people; machines don't require all the protection and **sustenance** that people do. And they are much easier to keep **operational** under harsh conditions. When NASA sent the robotic explorers *Spirit* and *Opportunity* to Mars a few years ago, they were expected to survive 90 days. More than three years later, they were still sending useful data back to Earth. A human mission may do some things that a robotic one cannot, but outlasting its planned stay is not one of them.

Should we establish a permanent base on the moon? Yes. Should it be a cooperative international effort? Yes. Should human beings be sent on exploration missions from this new base? No. In this case, we should let machines make our giant leap.

One of NASA's twin robots on Mars

**operational** (ahp-uh-RAY-shu-nuhl) being in working order

**sustenance** (SUS-tuh-nens) something that maintains life; nourishment

## THINK CRITICALLY

Do you agree with the author's argument in favor of robotic space explorers over human explorers? Explain your answer.

_____

_____

_____

## Compare and Contrast

The author of this persuasive essay argues that sending robots to a permanent base on the moon makes more sense than sending people there.

Complete the Venn diagram below to show the similarities and differences between robots and people at a permanent base on the moon. Write at least two details in each part of the diagram.

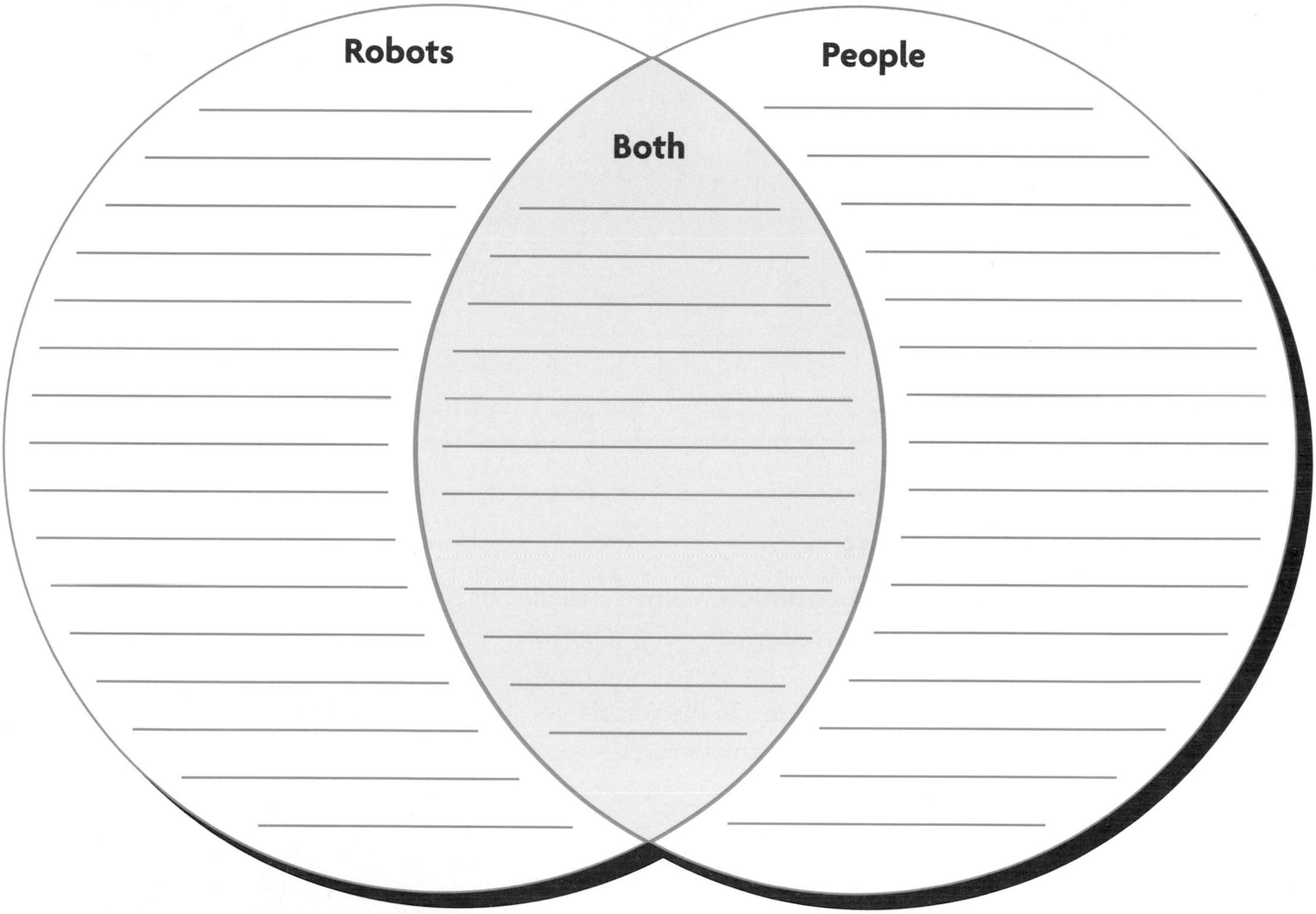

**Robots**          **People**

**Both**

### THINK CRITICALLY

Do you think a permanent base on the moon will ever become a reality? Why or why not?

_____

_____

_____

FOR A ROBOTIC
MOON BASE

## Summarize

You can summarize "For a Robotic Moon Base" by including each argument and your own thoughts about those arguments.

Reread the essay. Then, on the lines below, write the author's argument that is included in each section of the essay. Next, write your thoughts about the author's argument.

**What Model Should Be Used?**
Main Argument: _____
Your Thoughts: _____
**For Which Purposes?**
Main Argument: _____
Your Thoughts: _____
**Why Permanent?**
Main Argument: _____
Your Thoughts: _____
**Why Robots?**
Main Argument: _____
Your Thoughts: _____

## Identify Facts and Opinions

Many people have strong opinions. An **opinion** is a personal idea or belief about a topic. Unlike a fact, an opinion cannot be proved by checking a reliable source.

Below are three statements from the article. On the line before each statement write **F** if it is a fact or **O** if it is an opinion.

_____ Antarctica should be our model for a moon base.

_____ The moon's gravity is much weaker than Earth's gravity.

_____ NASA sent the robotic explorers *Spirit* and *Opportunity* to Mars in 2004.

_____ A permanent base on the moon should be a cooperative, international effort.

View of Earth as seen from the moon's surface

## Make Connections

Think about "Space Garden" and "For a Robotic Moon Base." Answer the following questions that connect the two selections to each other and to you.

1. Both selections are about going to space for scientific experiments. How did reading one selection help you better understand the other?

_____

_____

_____

_____

2. Think about Jorge's job in the story. Would he agree with the author's arguments in the persuasive essay? Explain your answer.

_____

_____

_____

_____

3. What information in the selections had the strongest effect on your opinion of space missions? Why?

_____

_____

_____

_____

4. If you were sent to work on the moon base, would you rather work with humans or with robots? Explain.

_____

_____

_____

_____

## Write a Persuasive Letter

Write a letter to your state representative in Congress, expressing your opinions about the space program. Support your opinions with examples.

Dear _____,

_____

_____

_____

_____

_____

_____

_____

Sincerely yours,

_____

**BLACKLINE MASTER** Before you write, use the Blackline Master your teacher will give you to plan your persuasive letter.

## Plan Your Research

What else would you like to know about space exploration? Write three questions you would like to research. Use books and the Internet to find answers.

1. _____

_____

2. _____

_____

3. _____

_____

**WEB CONNECTION**

http://www.OptionsPublishing.com/BestPracticesH

# NAVAJO LESSONS

Celine's plans for the summer change when her parents send her and her brother to visit Grandmother on the reservation. Will the visit be worthwhile, even though she can't speak Navajo?

## Recognize Genre

A **fiction** story is made up by an author. **Realistic fiction** is a story that could actually happen. The setting may be a place you've never seen, and the characters may do unexpected things. But if the setting, the characters, and the plot are possible, then the story is realistic fiction.

Think about what you know about realistic fiction. Circle **T** for true or **F** for false next to each statement.

**T  F**  The characters have special powers.

**T  F**  The setting could be a real place.

**T  F**  The characters' actions are believable.

**T  F**  The story could really happen.

Write one event that could happen in a realistic fiction story.

_____

_____

## Connect to the Topic

Ask yourself: *What do I know about the Navajo or other Native Americans?* Write what you know in the web below.

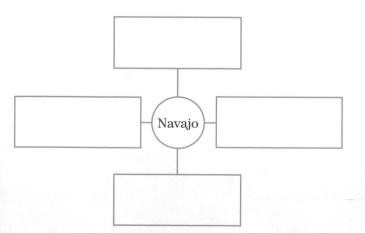

Navajo

## Preview and Predict

Reread the introduction. Then scan the story. Think about the title, the illustrations, and your word web. Predict two events that may happen in "Navajo Lessons."

**1.** _____

_____

_____

**2.** _____

_____

_____

# ◆NAVAJO LESSONS◆

**VISUALIZE**

You'll enjoy a story more if you imagine the setting as you read.

How do you imagine the setting in the first two paragraphs?

**UNDERSTAND GENRE**

(realistic fiction)
In realistic fiction, the characters act or think like real people.

How is Grandmother like a real person?

The van had been jolting over the rocky, dirt road for more than an hour. "My teeth will fall out if we drive another mile," Celine thought bitterly.

She couldn't believe her grandmother lived so far away from everything. Even more unbelievable was the fact that her parents were making her and Josh spend the whole summer on the Navajo reservation in northern Arizona. Celine had planned a great summer—early morning runs with Dora to get in shape for track; days at the pool with her friends; evenings at the Teen Center, dancing, laughing, and having fun.

Then Mom had gotten a letter from Aunt Billie. Cousin Sonia was getting ready to have her *Kinaaldá*, the Navajo girl's coming-of-age ceremony. Everyone was so excited. There would be a big, family party. Mom had gotten that faraway look in her eyes, the look that said, "What have we given up by moving off the reservation? We live so far away from our family." So Mom and Dad had decided to send Celine and Josh to their grandmother's house for the whole summer.

"Grandmother misses you two," Mom had said. "It would be good for both of you to spend time with her."

Finally, the van pulled up to the **hogan**. Celine had been there before. She knew to expect a dirt floor, no electricity, no running water, and few pieces of furniture.

"*Yá'át'ééh*," Grandmother greeted them. She knew few words of English. The plan was that Celine and Josh would learn Navajo by necessity. If they wanted to talk to anyone but each other, they'd have to speak Grandmother's language.

**DID YOU KNOW?**

During the four-day *Kinaaldá* ceremony, participants sing, run, eat corncakes, and do special activities that welcome a girl into womanhood.

**hogan** (HOH-gun) traditional Navajo home, made of earth and wood

Celine got through the first few days by pointing and grunting and by listening to her favorite music all day and night.

Josh was having a great time. He asked questions about everything. He'd point at something, and Grandmother would say a word. Josh would say it back, and Grandmother would laugh and say it again, correcting his **intonation**. Then Josh would repeat the word over and over until Celine thought she would scream.

Josh had even managed to find other human life out there. Granted, it was one mile away. Navajos didn't like to crowd one another. But Josh didn't mind the hike down to the Begay hogan. There were two boys his age, and the three of them were out all day **jabbering** away in Navajo and chasing one another up and down the **arroyos**.

Celine had picked up one Navajo word, *Shíká'anilyeed*—help. It was all she heard all day long. "*Shíká'anilyeed.*" Grandmother would point to the pot on the stove that needed stirring. "*Shíká'anilyeed.*" She also asked Celine to take the sheep out to graze.

It wasn't all work, though. Grandmother had a way of saying "Celine" that brimmed with affection. Every night, after they had snuggled into their sleeping bags, Grandmother began a long tale.

"What's she saying?" Celine would whisper to Josh.

"Shh, it's a story about Great-grandfather. He was a Code Talker in World War II. They helped win the war against Japan."

By the time Grandmother finished her story, Josh would be asleep, and Celine would still be in the dark about Great-grandfather's adventures.

## THINK CRITICALLY

Josh seems to be having a good time. How do you think Celine feels about that? What makes you think so?

_____

_____

_____

MAKE CONNECTIONS

Connect events in the story to what you already know.

I know that sometimes siblings don't get along. I can tell Celine is annoyed by Josh because she says she feels like screaming.

Josh is enjoying the visit. Tell about a time you experienced something new that you enjoyed.

_____

_____

_____

_____

How might you feel if you couldn't communicate with someone who spoke a different language?

_____

_____

_____

_____

**arroyos** (uh-ROY-ohz) dry river beds

**intonation** (in-toh-NAY-shun) changes in high and low sounds in spoken language

**jabbering** (JAB-ur-ing) talking rapidly

Ask yourself questions when an idea or word meaning is not clear. Look for help in events that happen before and after the word appears.

What does Shimásání mean? The only other person at the hogan is Grandmother. Shimásání must mean "Grandmother" in Navajo.

Celine "prompted" her relatives to say it again. What does "prompted" mean here?

_____

_____

_____

_____

To answer some questions, you may need to check outside resources.

Write one question you have that isn't answered in the story.

_____

_____

_____

Celine went running every morning. Even if she couldn't train with Dora, she would be ready for track when school started. One morning as she was returning to the hogan, Josh met up with her. His face was **stricken** and he was holding back tears.

"*Shimásání* is sick," he sobbed. "What are we going to do?"

Celine sprinted back to the hogan. Grandmother was lying on her side. Celine heard Grandmother's shallow breathing and bravely fought her own feeling of panic. "We've got to get help," said Celine. "You stay here with her. I'm going to run over to the Begays. They have a pickup truck, right?"

Josh nodded.

"You'll be all right, Josh. I'll be back soon."

Could she run fast enough? Would the truck be there? What would she say?

The Begay hogan came into view, and there was the truck.

"Hello, hello," she shouted. And then the words came to her. "*Shíká'anilyeed. Shimásání. Shíká'anilyeed.*" "Help. Grandmother. Help." The Begay grandfather was home. They made the drive back to Grandmother's hogan in silence. There they lifted her gently into the back of the pickup. Celine and Josh rode with her, shading her from the sun.

A few hours later, they were in the hospital in Tuba City, surrounded by concerned relatives. "You did the right thing," they told Celine. "Because of you, she got here in time. You run fast, like the **Diné**," they told her in English.

"Say it again," Celine prompted. "Say it in Navajo."

**Diné** (dee-NEH) Navajo word meaning "the people," which is what the Navajos call themselves

**stricken** (STRIK-uhn) affected by distress

# UNDERSTANDING FICTION

## NAVAJO LESSONS

## Analyze Characters

An important feature of "Navajo Lessons" is the realistic characterizations of Celine and Josh. Like any sister and brother, the two have similarities and differences. Use the Venn diagram to compare the two characters.

**Celine**

**Both**

**Josh**

### THINK CRITICALLY

Think about Celine's thoughts and feelings throughout the story. Explain how and why she changed by the end of the story.

## Summarize

A good summary tells all the important information and leaves out less important details.

   Fill in the bubble next to the best summary of "Navajo Lessons."

Ⓐ Celine and Josh travel to the Navajo reservation in a van. They're there for their cousin's party. Josh makes friends but Celine doesn't. Grandmother becomes sick, and they take her to the hospital in Tuba City.

Ⓑ Celine and her brother Josh spend a summer with their grandmother on the Navajo reservation. Josh learns Navajo and makes friends. Celine listens to her CD player and runs. At night, Grandmother tells stories about Great-grandfather. He was a Code Talker in World War II. The Begay grandfather has a pickup truck.

Ⓒ Celine and her brother Josh spend a summer with their grandmother on the Navajo reservation. Josh starts to learn Navajo, but Celine isn't interested. When Grandmother becomes sick, Celine must use the few Navajo words she has learned to get help. Afterward, she is more interested in learning Navajo.

How did you decide which two answers are NOT correct?

_____

_____

_____

_____

## Identify Theme

Often a character in a story changes because of something he or she has learned. That "lesson" is the theme of the story, or the message that the author wants readers to remember.

   Answer these questions to help you understand and write the theme of "Navajo Lessons."

**1.** How does Celine feel at the beginning of the story?

_____

**2.** What does she say at the end of the story?

_____

**3.** How have her feelings changed by the end of the story?

_____

**4.** What event caused her feelings to change?

_____

**5.** What is the theme, or author's message?

_____

# HUMAN CODE MACHINE

Navajo Code Talkers helped the United States win important battles in the Pacific Ocean during World War II. What did these courageous men do that no one else could have done?

## Recognize Genre

As you know, an **informational article** is a type of **nonfiction** that gives facts about a topic. The author's purpose is to present information in an interesting and understandable way.

Informational articles often have features that show how the material is organized and help you understand the material better. Look quickly through "Human Code Machine." Then put a check next to each feature contained in the article.

- [ ] headings that divide the topic into smaller subtopics
- [ ] cartoon illustrations
- [ ] visuals such as drawings, charts, graphs, and maps that show something about the topic
- [ ] photographs and captions

How might these features help you better understand the text?

## Connect to the Topic

Read the introduction to "Human Code Machine." Ask yourself: *What do I know about Navajos? What do I know about World War II?* Write one thing you know about each topic.

Navajos:_____

_____

World War II:_____

_____

## Preview and Predict

You've read the title and introduction and have glanced at the article. Predict what you will learn.

_____

_____

_____

_____

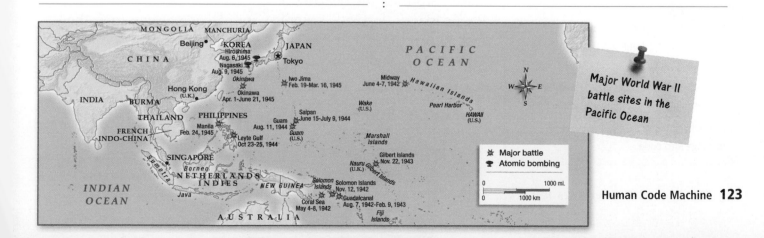

Major World War II battle sites in the Pacific Ocean

★ Major battle
☢ Atomic bombing

# HUMAN CODE MACHINE

## MAKE INFERENCES

When reading nonfiction, use what you have read and what you know to make inferences, or figure out things that are not explained.

What inference can you make about code machines?

_____

_____

_____

_____

_____

_____

_____

_____

_____

Bullets and shells tore through the air as U.S. Marines hit the beach. On the sands of Iwo Jima Island, any other World War II code machine would have been too slow to use in the heat of battle. But the Marines had highly mobile **cryptographs**, each with two arms, two legs, and an unbreakable code.

From the first day's invasion to the final battle a month later, the human code machines kept messages crackling over military radios. *Gini*, the code said. *Behnaalitsosie. Neasjah. Lotso.* Throughout the combat, more mysterious words filled the airwaves. Finally, as a photographer took the famous picture of the American flag flying over Mt. Suribachi, the news went out in Navajo.

*Naastosi Thanzie Dibeh Shida Dahnestsa Tkin Shush Wollachee Moasi Lin Achi.*

Ordinary Marines listening to this babble were as baffled as Japanese soldiers intercepting the messages. Had they spoken Navajo, they would have recognized the words: Mouse, Turkey, Sheep, Uncle, Ram, Ice, Bear, Ant, Cat, Horse, Intestines.

But what could these words mean? To the Navajo Code Talkers, the first letter of each word spelled out Mt. Suribachi. Other code filled in the announcement: Iwo Jima was under American control.

From 1942 to 1945, more than four-hundred Navajo Code Talkers stormed the beaches of Pacific islands. Instantly **encoding** and **decoding** messages, they helped win the war in the Pacific. Even today, their code remains one of the few in history that was never broken.

### DID YOU KNOW?

The Navajo were not the first Native American code talkers. A small group of Choctaw men encoded military messages during World War I.

**cryptographs** (KRIP-tuh-grafs) devices for solving things written in code

**decoding** (dee-KOHD-ing) figuring out the meaning of something written in code

**encoding** (en-KOHD-ing) converting a message into code

Two soldiers, who are also cousins, relay orders in their native Navajo language.

Navajos serving wih a Marine Signal Unit, operating a portable radio set in a dense jungle close to the front lines

**MAKE CONNECTIONS**
As you read, connect what you read to your own experiences.

Describe a time when you heard someone speak in a language that you didn't understand.

_____

_____

_____

When reading nonfiction, make connections between information you already know and new ideas in your reading.

In Navajo, the word for "chicken hawk" became "dive bomber." I know that a dive bomber dives straight down to hit its target. So, a chicken hawk must also dive straight down.

What is the connection between "Lotso" and battleship?

_____

_____

_____

## The Mystery Language

When World War II began, hundreds of Navajo men volunteered to fight. Most had never been off of their reservation, a high, **barren** plain stretching across Arizona, Utah, and New Mexico. Most Navajo spoke some English, but the business of their daily lives was conducted in their own language.

Among Native-American languages, Navajo was the one least likely to be known to foreigners. The language was entirely oral. Not a single book had ever been written in Navajo.

The Navajo code was **proposed** by a non-Navajo, Philip Johnston, the son of missionaries on the reservation. Marine officers were **skeptical** at first. At Camp Elliott, north of San Diego, California, Johnston arranged a test. "Translate some messages from Navajo to English and back again," he told some old friends. As Marines listened in, their faces went **slack**. The words were not encoded, yet top cryptographers had no hope of **deciphering** them. Navajo itself was a mystery, even without a code. Soon, the Marines went looking for what they now call "a few good men" fluent in both English and Navajo.

## Making a Code

The Navajo language didn't contain many words used in war, such as *bomber*, *battleship*, and *grenade*. In making their code, the Navajo soldiers rooted it in nature. They named military planes after birds. *Gini*, Navajo for "chicken hawk," became "dive bomber." They named ships after fish. *Lotso*, meaning "whale," was the code word for "battleship."

To spell out proper names, the Code Talkers encoded a Navajo zoo. Marines spell out abbreviations with their own alphabet, which begins *Able*, *Baker*, *Charlie*. The Navajo version began *Wollachee*, *Shush*, *Moasi*, meaning *Ant*, *Bear*, *Cat*.

**barren** (BAHR-in) empty

**deciphering** (dee-SIE-fer-ing) translating a code into ordinary language

**proposed** (proh-POHZD) suggested

**skeptical** (SKEP-tuh-kuhl) doubtful; questioning

**slack** (slak) dull; expressionless

## UNDERSTAND GENRE
(informational article)
The author started this article in the middle of an explanation and then went back to the beginning.

In time order, what part of the article would have come first? Write the heading and the first sentence of this new beginning below.

**Heading:** _____

_____

**First sentence:** _____

_____

_____

Why does the "Recognition at Last" section look different from the others?

_____

_____

_____

_____

_____

## Test Time

With just 400 words encoded, the Navajo handed a message to Navy intelligence officers, who spent three weeks trying and failing to decipher it. Then, armed with a code and M-1 rifles, a few dozen Code Talkers shipped out to the Pacific. Two remained behind to teach the code to other Navajo recruits.

On Guadalcanal, Code Talkers had to prove themselves again. Officers staged a race, **pitting** Code Talkers against a mechanical cryptograph that was sending a message through the jungle. The Code Talkers won the race handily. They were ready for battle.

On the island of Saipan, an advancing American battalion was shelled from behind by its own troops. Desperate messages called, "Hold your fire!" But since the Japanese were imitating Marine broadcasts, no one knew whether the cry was real. Then headquarters asked, "Do you have a Navajo?" A single Navajo sent the same message just once, and the shelling stopped.

Between invasions, the Code Talkers **convened** to encode new battle terms. They transmitted thousands of messages without error. Before the war ended, several were killed in action. In a language that needed no decoding, Marine Major Howard Conner assessed their contribution. "Without the Navajos," Conner said, "the Marines would never have taken Iwo Jima."

### Recognition at Last

For decades after World War II, the public knew nothing about the work of the Navajo Code Talkers. Finally, in 1969, the Code Talkers of the 4th Marine Division were publicly honored at a reunion with a medal **commemorating** their service. Two years later, President Richard Nixon issued Certificates of Appreciation to all of the Code Talkers.

Since then, several other **testimonials** to their efforts have been created. The Pentagon building in Washington, D.C., now displays a permanent Code Talker exhibit. The National Code Talkers Association, which has less than thirty surviving members, also set up a Code Talkers Museum in Gallup, New Mexico.

A bronze sculpture in Phoenix, Arizona, honors Navajo Code Talkers who served during World War II.

**commemorating** (kuh-MEM-uh-rayt-ing) recognizing; celebrating

**convened** (kuhn-VEEND) met; assembled

**pitting** (PIT-ing) setting up in a contest

**testimonials** (tes-tuh-MOH-nee-ulz) statements of praise

**HUMAN CODE MACHINE**

## Identify Problem and Solution

"Human Code Machine" describes the solution to a problem faced by the United States military during World War II. Check your understanding of the article by completing this chart. The problem is not stated directly in the article, so you will need to infer what it is.

*If I work backwards and first think about the results and then think about the actions that caused the results, I should figure out the problem.*

**Problem:**

**Actions Taken to Solve Problem:**

**Results:**

### THINK CRITICALLY

Review your chart. What are the advantages of using "human code machines"? What are some disadvantages?

_____

_____

_____

## Summarize

To summarize the important information in an article, ask and answer these questions:
*Who? What? When? Where? Why? How?*

Answer the following questions for "Human Code Machine."

Who? _____

What happened? _____

_____

When? _____

Where? _____

Why? _____

_____

How? _____

_____

## Identify Details

The visuals in an article can help you determine what important ideas
you should remember.

For each visual in "Human Code Machine," write one important
idea that it represents.

Veterans from New Mexico are recognized for their service to the country.

**1.** Statue of flag-raising on Iwo Jima (page 124):

_____

_____

**2.** Map (page 123): _____

_____

_____

**3.** Code talkers (page 124 and 125): _____

_____

_____

**4.** Statue honoring code talkers (page 126): _____

_____

_____

## Make Connections

When you read nonfiction, you are adding to your knowledge of the world you live in. Think of what you knew about Navajo culture before reading the selections and what you learned from reading "Navajo Lessons" and "Human Code Machine." Complete the chart below.

### Navajo Culture

| What I know | What I learned from "Navajo Lessons" | What I learned from "Human Code Machine" |
|---|---|---|
| | | |

How does reading one selection help you understand the other selection?

_____

_____

_____

_____

## Plan an Interview

Imagine you could interview one of the surviving Navajo Code Talkers. Think about questions you would like to ask him. Write them on the lines below, along with statements of the purpose and focus of your interview.

Purpose: _____

_____

Focus: _____

_____

Questions: _____

_____

_____

_____

_____

_____

_____

**BLACKLINE MASTER** Before you write, use the Blackline Master your teacher will give you to plan your interview.

## Plan Your Research

What else would you like to know about Navajo culture or the Navajo Code Talkers? Write three questions on the lines below. Research the answers by using print or online resources.

1. _____

_____

2. _____

_____

3. _____

_____

**WEB CONNECTION**

http://www.OptionsPublishing.com/BestPracticesH

## Sacagawea Saves the Day

This part of the lesson is a test. After you read "Sacagawea Saves the Day," you will answer questions about the selection. These questions will test how well you understand the reading strategies you have practiced.

Sacagawea, a young woman with a small baby strapped to her back, was the only woman on a difficult journey through the wilderness. Read to learn about how her own experiences help the men on the expedition and keep her calm when a storm threatens them.

## Recognize Genre

"Sacagawea Saves the Day" is an **historical fiction** story. It blends facts and fictional details. Think about other historical fiction you have read. On the lines below, write two things you expect to find in historical fiction.

1. _____

_____

_____

_____

2. _____

_____

_____

_____

## Connect to the Topic

Reread the introduction to "Sacagawea Saves the Day." Ask yourself: *What do I know about Sacagawea? What do I know about the journey she went on?* Write two things you know on the lines below.

1. _____

_____

_____

2. _____

_____

_____

## Preview and Predict

Scan the story. Think about the title and illustrations. Think about what you wrote about the topic. Then make a prediction.

This story will be about _____

_____

_____

_____ .

Sacagawea Saves the Day

The young woman sat quietly near the back of the boat with her baby strapped to her back in a **cradleboard**. "Sweet little Pomp," she thought. The name meant "first born" in her first language. His father insisted on calling him Jean-Baptiste, but Sacagawea (sah-kuh-juh-WEE-uh) knew that her son would always be more Shoshone (show-SHOW-nee) than French. He was such a good child, just three months old and already a contented traveler.

Sacagawea looked back at her husband, Charbonneau (shar-boh-NOH). The Frenchman was hard to live with, but, she thought, where would she be now if they hadn't married? Without a doubt, she would be back at the Hidatsa (hee-DAHT-sah) village, where she had spent the last five years since a Hidatsa raiding party had captured her and taken her on a long journey away from her people.

Instead, she and Charbonneau were traveling west with the white men, who said they were going all the way to the big water. They had told Charbonneau that they hoped to find Shoshone and trade with them for horses. They would need horses to take them over the high mountains before the snows came. They thought Sacagawea could help them talk with her people. Well, she would be happy to do that for a chance to see her friends and family again.

> **cradleboard** (CRAY-duhl-bord) stiff frame used for carrying an infant

Charbonneau had hold of the stick that steered the boat while the rowers and the wind in the sail moved it forward. The two leaders were on the shore watching the boat's progress. The one they called Lewis never had much to say to her. But the other one, Clark, with the hair like flames, smiled often, called her boy "Pompey," and had even given her a nickname. Janey, he called her. She didn't know why. He just seemed glad to have her in the party of 33 men.

They should be very glad I am here, Sacagawea thought. These men were helpless when it came to finding food in the woods. They overlooked the most obvious roots and stalks. Already, they had been pleased with the tasty treats she had unearthed.

A sudden chill came over Sacagawea and interrupted her thoughts. The sky had darkened and the wind was whipping the river into **whitecaps**. She glanced back at Charbonneau. He looked frightened, but then he was always nervous on the water. She was glad Cruzatte was in the boat. At least he knew what he was doing.

Suddenly, the wind turned the boat. They were headed toward the shore now, and everyone was shouting at once. In an instant, the boat was on its side and water was pouring in. It was three-hundred yards to the shore. Could she fight the **current** with Pomp on her back? No, better to stay with the boat.

Charbonneau let go of the steering stick and raised his hands to the sky. Fear was in his eyes. "Why can't he figure out how to save himself and the rest of them?" thought Sacagawea.

**current** (KUR-uhnt) strong flow of water
**whitecaps** (WITE-kaps) waves with their tops broken into white foam

Cruzatte, his eyes blazing, was shouting at Charbonneau. Sacagawea didn't know what Cruzatte said, but he must have scared her husband more than the water did because the terrified man had grabbed the steering stick again.

Sacagawea looked around. Bundles of supplies, books and instruments were floating in the water. Lewis and Clark treasured those things. She had seen them **pore** over the pages with unfamiliar markings and pictures of the night sky. She had watched them consult their instruments before setting off in a certain direction to hunt.

Without a moment's hesitation, she reached out and grabbed the nearest bundle. The cradleboard shifted on her back, throwing her off balance, but she knew Pomp was secure in it. She struggled with the bundle and got it into the boat. Another package floated nearby. Again, she reached out. Over and over, she pulled the precious bundles out of the water.

Finally, the boat began to right itself. Following Cruzatte's instructions, Charbonneau had managed to get it under control. Cruzatte ordered two men to start **bailing** while he and two others rowed toward the shore. Sacagawea continued to **pluck** packages out of the water. In this fashion, the boat pulled up to the shore, barely afloat.

Captain Lewis, who had witnessed the **mishap** from where he stood on shore, looked happier than she had ever seen him. With much gratitude, he gave her a hand out of the boat before turning to scold Charbonneau.

It was Clark who relieved the tension.

"Janey," he said, "you have saved the day." And he gave her a big grin.

**bailing** (BAYL-ing) removing water from a boat by filling and emptying a container

**mishap** (MISS-hap) bad luck; an unfortunate accident

**pluck** (PLUK) snatch; grab

**pore** (PORE) read or study carefully

Use what you have read to answer questions 1–9.

## Multiple Choice

1. "Sacagawea Saves the Day" is an historical fiction story because it includes

   (A) graphic aids.

   (B) information organized by headings.

   (C) facts about a real person.

   (D) actual photos taken at the time.

2. Which statement **best** describes Charbonneau based on his behavior on the river?

   (A) He likes adventure on the water.

   (B) He is a devoted father.

   (C) He is an experienced sailor.

   (D) He is a fearful and nervous sailor.

3. What might have happened differently in the story if Sacagawea hadn't been on the boat when it tipped on its side?

   (A) Charbonneau would have been more capable of steadying the boat.

   (B) Some of Lewis and Clark's books and instruments might have been lost.

   (C) Captain Lewis would have rescued everyone.

   (D) The river water wouldn't have gotten so rough.

4. Which sentence helps you **best** visualize the scene just before the boat tips on its side?

   (A) The sky is gray and the water is very rough.

   (B) The sky is sunny and a strong wind is blowing.

   (C) The sky is dark and the water is deadly still.

   (D) The sky is gray and rain is falling.

5. Which event is **most** important to the story's plot?

   (A) Everyone in the boat was shouting at once.

   (B) The baby in the cradleboard on Sacagawea's back threw her off balance.

   (C) Sacagawea and Charbonneau were traveling west with the white men.

   (D) Sacagawea unearthed tasty treats for the men.

6. Why did Lewis and Clark's group need horses to get over the high mountains?

   (A) Horses would keep the group from getting lost because horses know where to go.

   (B) Horses were the least expensive form of transportation.

   (C) The baby would be more comfortable on a horse.

   (D) Horses were the best form of transportation because there was no water route.

7. Which sentence **best** states the theme, or message, of the story?

   (A) It's always more fun to travel in groups.

   (B) Staying calm and focused during a time of trouble helps you solve a problem.

   (C) Knowing another language is important for traveling.

   (D) Always be prepared for rough waters.

8. Why was Sacagawea an important member of the group traveling with Lewis and Clark?

   (A) She was the best cook.

   (B) She was an excellent sailor.

   (C) She could take care of their books and instruments.

   (D) She was the only one who could speak the Shoshone language.

## Short Response

9. Explain two ways things would be different for the Lewis and Clark group if Sacagawea hadn't been traveling with them. Use details from the story to support your response.

_____

_____

_____

_____

_____

_____

_____

_____

_____

_____

_____

_____

_____

_____

**STOP** This is the end of the test for "Sacagawea Saves the Day." When your teacher tells you, go on to read the next selection, "On the Lewis and Clark Trail."

ON THE LEWIS AND CLARK TRAIL

This part of the lesson is a test. After you read "On the Lewis and Clark Trail," you will answer questions about the selection. These questions will test how well you understand the reading strategies you have practiced.

From 1804 to 1806, a Shoshone woman named Sacagawea accompanied the Lewis and Clark expedition across the uncharted wilderness of the American West. Today, the Lewis and Clark National Historic Trail can take you through some of the same territory.

## Recognize Genre

An **informational article** is a type of **nonfiction** that presents facts about a topic. Informational articles often include certain features. Take a quick look at "On the Lewis and Clark Trail." Which features does it contain? Check each one that you find in the article.

_____ chart          _____ instructions

_____ map            _____ captions

_____ headings       _____ photographs

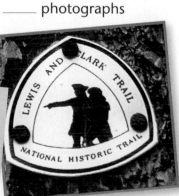

Lewis and Clark Trail marker, Lolo Pass, Bitterroot Mountains, Montana

## Connect to the Topic

Reread the introduction to "On the Lewis and Clark Trail." Ask yourself: *What did I learn about Sacagawea and the Lewis and Clark expedition from reading "Sacagawea Saves the Day?"* On the lines below, write two things you learned.

1. _____

_____

_____

2. _____

_____

_____

## Preview and Predict

Now that you have looked at the article, think about the title and the features. Make a prediction. Tell what you think you will learn as you read "On the Lewis and Clark Trail."

_____

_____

_____

_____

_____

**On the Lewis and Clark Trail 137**

ON THE LEWIS AND CLARK TRAIL

Portrait of William Clark

You can fly from St. Louis, Missouri, to Astoria, Oregon, in about five hours. Or, you can follow in the footsteps of explorers Lewis and Clark and travel 3,700 miles up the Missouri River, across the Rocky Mountains, and down the Columbia River to the Pacific coast. For speed, take an airplane, but for fun you might want to visit some spots along the Lewis and Clark National Historic Trail.

## The Corps of Discovery

In 1803, the United States purchased the Louisiana Territory from France. Much of this huge expanse of land was wilderness, known only to the Native Americans who lived there. President Thomas Jefferson wanted to know what the land and its animals and plants were like and if there was a water route that would lead to the Pacific Ocean. He also wanted to establish friendly relations with the Native Americans.

Portrait of Meriwether Lewis

Jefferson asked his trusted secretary, Meriwether Lewis, to lead an expedition. Lewis enlisted William Clark as his co-leader. Together, they assembled the **Corps** of Discovery. Thirty-three volunteers, mostly from the U.S. Army, gave more than two years of their lives for the adventure of a lifetime.

After months of planning, the Corps of Discovery set off from what is now Wood River, Illinois, on May 14, 1804. You can read the history of the expedition's remarkable adventure in the landscape of the Lewis and Clark Trail today. The trail, winding its way through parts of eleven states, lets you retrace portions of the journey by water, car, and on foot. Read ahead to learn about highlights of the trail.

**corps** (KORE) a branch of the military performing a specialized duty

Old Columbia River in Gorge, Oregon

# Up the Mighty Missouri

The expedition proceeded up the Missouri River by boat, stopping to meet with Native Americans wherever they found them. Near Sioux City, Iowa (1), you can visit a monument to Sergeant Charles Floyd, the only member of the Corps to die during the expedition, probably of a burst **appendix**. His comrades buried him on a rounded hill, which Lewis and Clark named Floyd's Bluff.

The expedition spent its first winter at Fort Mandan, which they built near a cluster of Mandan and Hidatsa villages in what is now central North Dakota. A reconstruction of the fort (2) is located about 12 miles south of the original site. Several miles north of that is the Knife River Indian Villages National Historic Site (3). Here you can see a film and exhibits about the Mandan and Hidatsa as well as a furnished reproduction of a Hidatsa earthen lodge.

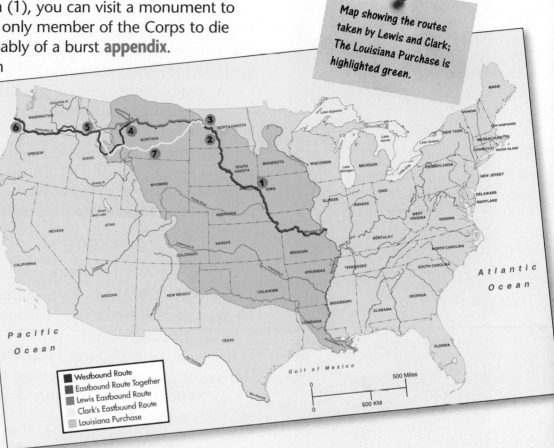

Map showing the routes taken by Lewis and Clark; The Louisiana Purchase is highlighted green.

In June of 1805, Lewis and Clark reached the Great Falls (4) of the Missouri River at what is now Great Falls, Montana. It took the expedition a month to carry six huge dugout canoes and many supplies 18 miles around the falls. At the Lewis and Clark National Historic Trail Interpretive Center in Great Falls, exhibits cover the whole Lewis and Clark journey. A hands-on exhibit called the Missouri River Mile-O-Meter lets you experience how difficult it was to haul the canoes upriver. At another exhibit you can hear the four-language translation chain Lewis had to use to bargain for horses with the Shoshone. (Lewis spoke English to Labiche, who translated into French for Charbonneau, who spoke in Hidatsa to Sacagawea, who translated into Shoshone for her people.)

**appendix** (uh-PEN-diks) an outgrowth of the large intestine; has no function, but if infected and bursts, can be fatal

## Across the Mountains to the Sea

When they reached the Rocky Mountains, the expedition followed the Lolo Trail (5) over the Bitterroot Range. They crossed some of the most rugged **terrain** in the mountains in freezing, wet weather and on starvation **rations**. Today, there are hiking trails that will give you a taste of the trip without the hardships endured during the expedition.

Eventually, the expedition reached the great Columbia River, where the men built canoes and rode the river to the Pacific Ocean. Winter was coming, so the men constructed Fort Clatsop (6) near what is now Astoria, Oregon. Near the original site stands a reconstruction of the fort, where costumed interpreters will answer your questions and let you test out Clark's bed or try on a buckskin jacket.

## Going Home

On March 23, 1806, the expedition headed home. About 28 miles east of present-day Billings, Montana, Clark climbed a 200-foot sandstone rock, which he named Pompey's Pillar (7) in honor of the expedition's youngest member. On a path leading to the top, Clark inscribed his name and the date. Today, at Pompey's Pillar National Historic Landmark, you can see the inscription and take a guided walk that covers local history, animals, and plants.

The expedition arrived in St. Louis on September 23, 1806. As Sergeant John Ordway wrote, "…the people of the town gathered on the bank and could hardly believe that it was us, for they had heard and had believed that we were all dead and were forgotten." And they have not been forgotten since. Just over two-hundred years later, their history-making journey can still be read in the landscape of the American West.

Lewis and Clark's trail over Lolo Pass, Bitterroot Mountain, Montana

**rations** (RASH-uhnz) food supplies
**terrain** (ter-AYN) ground

Use what you have read to answer questions 1–9.

## Multiple Choice

1. Which feature in the article helps you **best** understand the route that Lewis and Clark followed?

    (A) the photographs

    (B) the headings

    (C) the map

    (D) the captions

2. If the Corps of Discovery had the use of modern technology in 1804, the expedition would have been different in all of the following ways, except for

    (A) needing a translator to speak with the Shoshone.

    (B) a shorter amount of time required for travel.

    (C) easier methods for recording information.

    (D) easier ways to transport supplies.

3. When did Clark name a 200-foot sandstone rock "Pompey's Pillar" in honor of the expedition's youngest member?

    (A) on the journey home

    (B) on May 14, 1804

    (C) on September 23, 1806

    (D) when reaching the Rocky Mountains

4. The expedition traveled through "rugged terrain" in the Rocky Mountains. Which detail would you **not** picture as being in rugged terrain?

    (A) thorny bushes

    (B) steep, narrow trails

    (C) rocky cliffs

    (D) treeless flatlands

5. Which detail about the Lewis and Clark expedition would President Jefferson find **most** important for his needs?

    (A) The Mandan and Hidatsa were unfriendly to Lewis and Clark.

    (B) Lewis and Clark were careful about keeping accurate records of their journey.

    (C) Lewis and Clark would never forget Sacagawea.

    (D) The Corps of Discovery began its journey on May 14, 1804.

6. Why did Lewis and Clark **most** likely build Fort Mandan and Fort Clatsop?

    (A) They thought they had reached the end of their journey.

    (B) They could not travel during the winter.

    (C) Some members of the expedition did not want to return home.

    (D) They built forts as national historical landmarks.

**7.** Which sentence **best** states the main idea of the article?

Ⓐ The Lewis and Clark National Historic Trail goes through parts of eleven states both on land and water.

Ⓑ The Lewis and Clark National Historic Trail lets you follow the route of the Lewis and Clark expedition of 1804–1806.

Ⓒ Lewis and Clark assembled the Corps of Discovery.

Ⓓ When Lewis and Clark returned to St. Louis, they learned that people had been told they were dead.

**8.** Why is the Lewis and Clark expedition described in the article as a "history-making journey"?

Ⓐ Areas that were unknown to Americans at the time were explored, and careful maps and records of their journey were kept.

Ⓑ People can learn about the journey only in history books.

Ⓒ It was a journey that allowed the men to travel back in time.

Ⓓ No one had ever met Native Americans before the expedition.

## Short Response

**9.** Explain why the Lewis and Clark Expedition is important to American history. Use details from the article to support your response.

_____

_____

_____

_____

_____

_____

_____

_____

_____

_____

_____

_____

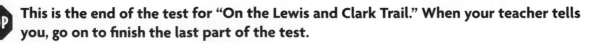

**STOP** **This is the end of the test for "On the Lewis and Clark Trail." When your teacher tells you, go on to finish the last part of the test.**

Use what you have read in both selections to answer questions 1–6.

## Multiple Choice

1. Which statement **best** compares the two selections?

   Ⓐ The selections are both historical fiction.

   Ⓑ The two selections are both about the Lewis and Clark expedition.

   Ⓒ Both selections focus on Sacagawea's contributions to the Lewis and Clark expedition.

   Ⓓ Both selections identify important spots along the Lewis and Clark Trail.

2. Which aspect of the expedition do both selections include?

   Ⓐ hardships encountered on the journey

   Ⓑ the personalities of Lewis and Clark

   Ⓒ the length of the journey

   Ⓓ the trek over the Rocky Mountains

3. Which detail is **not** included in both selections?

   Ⓐ Sacagawea accompanied Lewis and Clark on their journey.

   Ⓑ Lewis and Clark wanted to reach the Pacific Ocean.

   Ⓒ Sacagawea gave birth at Fort Mandan.

   Ⓓ Lewis and Clark needed to get horses from the Shoshone.

4. Which detail from the story helps you understand the name Clark gave to one of the historic sites in honor of the expedition's youngest member?

   Ⓐ Clark gave Sacagawea the nickname Janey.

   Ⓑ Sacagawea was married to a French man named Charbonneau.

   Ⓒ Sacagawea's son was named Pomp.

   Ⓓ The Shoshone would trade horses with Lewis and Clark.

5. Describe an historic site you have visited or seen in pictures. Compare and contrast it with one of the sites on the Lewis and Clark National Historic Trail.

   _____

   _____

   _____

   _____

   _____

   _____

   _____

   _____

   _____

   _____

   _____

**6.** Imagine that you were part of the Corps of Discovery. Write a journal entry to describe a day on the expedition. Use details from both selections to help you write your entry.

_____

_____

_____

_____

_____

_____

_____

_____

_____

_____

_____

_____

_____

_____

_____

_____

_____

_____

_____

_____

_____

_____

_____

_____

**STOP** **This is the end of the test.**